OPPORTUNITIES

in

Hotel and Motel Careers

D0019248

OPPORTUNITIES

in

Hotel and Motel Careers

REVISED EDITION

SHEPARD HENKIN

McGraw·Hill

New York   Chicago   San Francisco   Lisbon   London   Madrid   Mexico City
Milan   New Delhi   San Juan   Seoul   Singapore   Sydney   Toronto

The McGraw·Hill Companies

Library of Congress Cataloging-in-Publication Data

Henkin, Shepard.
    Opportunities in hotel and motel careers / by Shepard Henkin. — Rev. ed.
       p.   cm.
    ISBN 0-07-145870-0 (alk. paper)
    1. Hotel management—Vocational guidance.   2. Motel management—
Vocational guidance.   I. Title: Opportunities in hotel and motel careers.
II. Title.

    TX911.3.V62H46   2006
    647.94'068—dc22   2005016907

1 2 3 4 5 6 7 8 9 0   DOC/DOC   0 9 8 7 6

ISBN 0-07-145870-0

Interior design by Rattray Design

McGraw-Hill books are available at special quantity discounts to use as premiums and sales promotions, or for use in corporate training programs. For more information, please write to the Director of Special Sales, Professional Publishing, McGraw-Hill, Two Penn Plaza, New York, NY 10121-2298. Or contact your local bookstore.

This book is printed on acid-free paper.

Contents

Foreword   vii

1. An Overview of the Field   1

The hotel industry. Current trends. Hotels and the
community. Employment outlook. Income.

2. Education and Training   15

General education studies. Early preparation.
Apprenticeship and training. Career opportunities.
Personal attributes.

3. The Job Search   29

The American Hotel and Lodging Association.
Interviewing. Advancement.

4. **The Front of the House: Guest Services**   35

Service department. Hotel front office. Security
department. Banquet and catering department.

5. **The Front of the House: Business Departments
    and Management**   57

Accounting department. Credit department.
Purchasing department. Central files department.
Human resources department. Public relations and
advertising department. Sales and marketing
department. Operating management. Top
management.

6. **The Back of the House: Food Service,
    Housekeeping, and Maintenance**   87

The food service industry. Food and liquor
department. Housekeeping department. Additional
positions. Some final words.

Appendix A: Educational Programs in Hotel
    and Hospitality Management   107
Appendix B: Professional Associations   189
Appendix C: Periodicals   193

Foreword

WHEN THIS VERY useful volume was previously released, the world was a very different place. At the time, with a perspective of three decades in the hospitality industry, I had the privilege of offering some introductory thoughts that were reflective of both my attitude toward the industry and the state of the industry itself.

Without prolonging the discussions of why things have changed, let it be said that they have, and the hotel and motel portion of the hospitality industry has since become a very different place. Careers within that industry, still very challenging and gratifying, have changed as well.

Two intersecting forces have become tremendously influential in the past several years. If indications are correct, they will not only continue to dominate the travel and tourism industry on a global basis, but they will also continue to have a profound impact on the world of individual hoteliers.

First, we cannot dismiss the importance of being aware of the economic and financial forces at work in the industry. I am well aware that sentences that begin "In my day . . ." can have the immediate impact of creating generational barriers; but from an historical perspective (that may be a better way to say it), the hotel sector, unique as it was, seemed to have different financial rules. This is no longer the case.

Like any business intent on survival and success, ours is one that requires insight into the financial aspects of every facet and every detail. This is a business, and those who wish to enjoy both personal and professional success in the hospitality industry need to have more than a casual understanding of business and financial operations.

The second requirement for both engagement and advancement in hospitality as a career is possession of an authentic sense of . . . hospitality.

Our lives are filled with experiences that reveal the movement away from personal involvement and initiative. Pushing various buttons on command during a phone call to a "customer-service" line and hoping that something will eventually happen is one simple illustration. Facing a service employee across the counter and being told "There's nothing I can do" is another.

Those who would succeed in hospitality will approach the industry with an indomitable conviction that there *is* something you can do—and you'll find out how to do it.

The challenge for the next generation of hoteliers is to combine solid business skills with sincere and gracious hospitality. Not an easy task, but one I believe you will find very gratifying.

Those who will form and shape the industry in the years and decades ahead will need to understand the way the business works, how it can be profitable, and what opportunities lie ahead to revitalize the essential qualities of excitement, service, fulfillment, and personal satisfaction that the industry has to offer and can continue to provide.

I wish you my best and look forward to the day when you can look back on a career both successful and satisfying.

Darryl Hartley-Leonard
Former Chairman
Hyatt Hotels Corporation

1

An Overview of the Field

Hotels and motels are not only places where one can obtain good food and comfortable lodging; they are also centers of community life, with facilities for meetings, entertainment, communication, and personal services. Their stock in trade has always been hospitality and service, and hotels and motels have made an art of dispensing comfort, pleasing the palate, and creating an atmosphere of home for guests.

The Hotel Industry

Hotels and motels have been a part of the American scene since the earliest days of the country's history. From the simple roadside inns of the original colonies, which provided food and rest for weary travelers, to the modern steel and brick giants of today that are practically cities within cities, hotels and motels have been an integral part of every community.

The hotel industry has grown into a multinational giant from its humble beginnings, with new hotel chains forming every year. This is not just an American phenomenon; it is also common in Great Britain, Ireland, France, Japan, Singapore, Hong Kong, and almost every developed country. Most of our major hotels are part of international chains. This trend extends to other industries that have become part of the hospitality field, such as airlines, real estate firms, and financial organizations seeking investments.

Today, across America and worldwide, cities, towns, and villages are dotted with hotels and motels of every kind—from small, simple rooming houses to elaborate fully contained motels, skyscraper hotels, and sprawling resorts providing employment to thousands. In the United States alone, the hospitality industry is one of the largest, surpassed only by the automotive and food industries.

The hotel-motel industry is unusual among major industries in that it is comprised of a great variety of skilled and unskilled occupations. Many of these jobs are industry specific; others relate to various outside trades and professions. Those employed in the industry include chefs, managers, plumbers, carpenters, porters, bookkeepers, secretaries, engineers, salespeople, printers, telephone operators, elevator operators, upholsterers, painters, bellhops, accountants, cashiers, waiters, electricians, foreign language interpreters, security guards, public relations specialists, and scores of other workers.

Throughout this book we will analyze the occupations found in the larger hotel and motel operations because, for the most part, these jobs are duplicated in the smaller establishments. Depending on its size and locale, the small hotel or motel performs basically the same functions and services as the larger one, except for having a smaller, less-specialized staff.

However, keep in mind that although larger operations offer a greater number of opportunities, smaller establishments offer an excellent training ground for fundamental experience in overall hotel-motel operation. Remember, too, that although many beginning jobs do not require any special educational preparation, a broad education will improve your chances for advancement and give you the ability to perform many necessary duties outside your own sphere of experience.

The overall mission of the hotel industry is described by Dr. Robert A. Beck, former dean of the School of Hotel Administration, Cornell University, and a prominent industry consultant:

> The hospitality industry offers today's young men and young women a most interesting and exciting career. Management of a hotel or a restaurant calls for a wide range of capabilities. Guests must be received with cordiality and provided with comfortable, well-designed, and tastefully decorated surroundings. They need appetizing, wholesome food that has been wisely bought, properly stored, skillfully prepared, and graciously served. Various other conveniences in public areas, conference and exhibit rooms, communication systems, and travel services are required for proper guest service. Further, a staff of employees must be recruited, trained, and motivated to provide hospitable service. Moreover, all must be successfully coordinated to return a profit to the establishment's investors. For those wishing a rewarding and challenging life in service to their fellow man, a future in the hospitality field should certainly be considered.

Types of Hotels

There are many different kinds of hotels and motels. The three major types of hotel operations are commercial, residential, and resort. Commercial or transient hotels make up about three-fourths of the hotels in this country. According to 2003 statistics from the American Hotel and Lodging Association, The United States has over 47,500 lodging establishments with fifteen or more rooms, with a total of over 4.4 million guest rooms. Hotels and motels had annual sales of $105.3 billion.

These commercial or transient hotels cater to commercial travelers, including businesspeople, salespeople, and transient visitors—tourists who spend one or more nights at the hotel. Some of the guests may stay for longer periods, even though their essential business is still commercial. Commercial or transient hotels that operate public dining rooms and restaurants generally make these facilities available to the general public as well as to the hotel guests. Revenue from food business is an important part of many commercial hotel operations.

Another major source of revenue is the convention and meeting business. Newly built hotels are constructed with this in mind, and older hotels, when modernized, add public space facilities. Hotels and motels without these meeting and banquet rooms are at a competitive disadvantage.

Residential hotels make up about one-tenth of the total number of hotels in the United States. These hotels provide permanent and semipermanent quarters for guests. Most also provide food, and some have opened their dining rooms and restaurants to the public. In general, residential hotels are located in suburban or residential districts. But there are also numerous residential hotels located in or near business areas so as to provide their guests with swift and easy access to and from their businesses.

Resort hotels make up about one-sixth of the total number of hotels in this country. Resort hotel operation varies greatly depending on size and the hotel's distance from large urban centers. In some resort areas, the hotels are expected to provide only food and lodging, but many large resort hotels could not stay in business unless they also provided sport and meeting facilities. Some of the most famous resort hotels offer magnificent provisions for golf, tennis, swimming, boating, dancing, horseback riding, and planned social activities and entertainment.

Resorts also need to generate business to fill in when regular vacation business tapers off. For this reason many top resorts, especially those with large public spaces, solicit commercial business in the form of conventions, sales meetings, and incentive tours, especially during off-season periods. This is a major source of revenue.

Conference centers provide an additional source of business. Generally located in the suburbs, these fully self-contained centers provide state-of-the-art audiovisual and technical equipment and meet all physical requirements for business functions. Located where they are, they can ensure few or no distractions for corporate meetings.

Other Types of Lodging

In addition to hotels, the industry includes inns, tourist houses, tourist camps, motels, and rooming houses that also provide guests with lodging, and sometimes food.

Inns vary greatly in their appearance and type of operation. Some are huge, elaborate establishments that offer all the services provided by hotels; others are small and base their appeal on quaintness, unusual services, or decor. Many of these are bed-and-breakfast inns, which provide short-term lodging in private homes or small buildings converted for this purpose. In general, inns should be considered hotels. Their type of operation should be judged, as with hotels, by their size, local customs, and the mood, decor, atmosphere, or period they are planned to convey.

Tourist camps, which include cabins or trailer parks, grew up with the advent of the motor age. These camps must be located outside of city limits on or near highways with heavy traffic, and they cater to motorists in search of inexpensive lodging. Trailer parks are in themselves a major industry and, like the hotel industry, a growing one. Some tourist camps provide service stations and general stores. Service station operators started many of the original camps as sources of extra income. Many tourist camps offer employment opportunities primarily during the summer months, when travel is the heaviest.

The motel was adapted from the tourist camp. A deluxe version of the tourist camp, the motel has become more and more popular with travelers and is becoming an increasingly competitive threat to the hotel industry.

Motels today are as modern and as well equipped as hotels. In many instances, since they are newly constructed, motels are even better than their older hotel competition. Motels provide private baths, cable television and Internet connections, bellhop service, restaurants, telephone service, valet and laundry service, and they will even make reservations for you at your next stopping point. Other features sometimes make motels more convenient than hotels for motorists. Motels have parking lots so guests can park close to their rooms, thus saving money on garage bills and tipping, and they make unpacking and packing every night unnecessary.

Because of their locations along highways, at airports, and even in some downtown locations, motels constitute the greatest competition faced by hotels. These sites are chosen with an eye to highway and air traffic, as well as proximity to newly built industrial sections. The increase in highway and air travel has helped augment the growth of airport and highway motels, each new motel diverting a portion of the business that formerly went almost exclusively to downtown hotels.

Motels often have better locations than hotels built in former years and when different traffic patterns existed. In the early days of the hotel industry, hotels were built largely downtown and quite often near railroad stations. With the decrease of railroad passenger traffic and the move of both industry and offices to the suburbs, these downtown hotels are no longer convenient for the customers they once served.

The growing trend for businesses to establish suburban headquarters has led to another trend in motels. The companies that patronize suburban motels require public space for meetings and meals. In response to this need, many motels have added convention, meeting, and public ballroom space to their facilities. In this respect, motels offer strong competition to hotels for business accounts. Many hotel organizations consider this competition serious enough to enter the motel field themselves.

Another area of the industry is rooming houses. Rooming houses provide inexpensive lodging for weekly or monthly guests. Most people who choose a rooming house are attracted because of low rents and convenient access to transportation. Rooming houses that provide meals for their guests are called boardinghouses. These establishments do not provide the comforts of a hotel but merely the necessities, including room, linens, bath facilities (generally public), and maid service.

While not major in scope, another important type of hotel operation is the conversion of older hotels into senior citizen residences. Certain downtown hotels that have declined in popularity have been converted into housing for older people, who enjoy the easy access to downtown shopping and conveniences.

Current Trends

In recent years, lodging establishments affiliated with national chains have grown rapidly. This trend includes hotels, motels, camps, and recreational and RV parks. Familiar chain establishments represent dependability and quality at predictable rates to travelers. National corporations own many chains, while others are independently owned but affiliated with a chain through a franchise agreement.

Increases in competition and in the sophistication of travelers have induced the chains to provide lodging to serve a variety of customer budgets and accommodation preferences. In general, these lodging places may be grouped into four types of properties: luxury, all-suite, moderately priced, and economy accommodations. There is a steady increase in the number of limited-service or economy chain properties—e.g., economy lodging without lobbies, restaurants, lounges, and meeting rooms. These properties are not as costly to build and operate, and they appeal to budget-conscious family vacationers and travelers who are willing to sacrifice amenities for lower room prices.

While economy chains have become more prevalent, the movement in the hotel and lodging industry is toward more extended-stay properties. In addition to fully equipped kitchenettes and laundry services, extended-stay establishments offer guest amenities such as in-room access to the Internet and grocery shopping. This segment of the hotel and other accommodations industry has eliminated traditional hotel lobbies and twenty-four-hour personnel, and housekeeping is usually done only about once a week. This helps to keep costs to a minimum.

All-suite facilities, which are especially popular with business travelers, offer a living room and a bedroom. These accommodations are aimed at travelers who require lodging for extended stays, families traveling with children, and businesspeople needing to conduct small meetings without the expense of renting an additional room.

Increased competition among establishments in this industry has spurred many independently owned and operated hotels and other lodging places to join national or international reservation systems, which allow travelers to make multiple reservations for lodging, airlines, and car rentals with one telephone call. Nearly all hotel chains operate online reservation systems through the Internet.

Hotels and the Community

Because hotels* provide not only lodging and meals but also public rooms and space for meetings, much that is newsworthy takes place in hotels. Depending upon the size of the space available, meetings, conventions, luncheons, social events, charity affairs, and other activities of community and often national interest take place in hotels. Hotels perform a valuable community service by providing public meeting rooms. Public space in hotels allows many activities of local as well as general importance to take place in communities that would otherwise be unable to accommodate them.

Since the first hotel opened its doors to the public, hotels have been the setting for many of the most important local and national events. Civic and national functions usually take place in hotel ball-

---

* From this point on, we shall refer to all hotels, motels, resorts, and other lodging as hotels because the occupational information that follows applies generally to all of these establishments.

rooms, and famous visitors often stop over at the local hotel. Local celebrities, civic dignitaries, and community leaders can often be found at the hotel, having lunch or dinner, attending social or business functions, or attending civic or service club luncheons and meetings. Many groups hold regular meetings and luncheons at hotels.

If you plan to enter the hotel field, your future will always be exciting and interesting. Whether you work in a small or large hotel, in a small or large city, you will be in the midst of things if you are in the hotel business.

You may wonder why other halls or meeting places have not competed for their share of this business. Because of their long experience in the hospitality and food industries, hotels can offer service second to none in most communities. In larger cities, restaurants and some halls are providing competition, but few can match the prestige offered by a hotel.

Employment Outlook

Wage and salary employment in hotels and other accommodations is expected to increase by 17 percent through 2012, compared with 16 percent growth projected for all industries combined. Recently, business and leisure travelers have cut back on travel due to the weak economy and security concerns. However, travel should pick up as the economy improves and as people feel more comfortable about traveling again. In addition, as more states legalize some form of gambling, the hotel industry will increasingly invest in gaming, further fueling job growth.

Job opportunities should be concentrated in the largest hotel occupations, such as building cleaning workers and hotel, motel, and resort desk clerks. Many of these openings will occur in full-service hotels, resorts, and spas simply because they employ the most workers. Because all-suite properties and extended-stay and budget hotels and motels do not have restaurants, dining rooms, lounges, or kitchens, these limited-service establishments offer a narrower range of employment opportunities.

The employment outlook varies by occupation. Employment of hotel, motel, and resort desk clerks is expected to grow faster than some other occupations in the industry as some of these workers assume responsibilities previously reserved for managers. However, the spread of computer technology will cause employment of other clerical workers, such as bookkeeping, accounting, and auditing clerks and secretaries, to grow more slowly than employment in the industry as a whole. Employment of waiters and waitresses also will grow more slowly, reflecting the growing number of hotels and other accommodations that do not offer full-service restaurants. Similarly, employment of lodging managers will not grow as fast due to the growth of economy-class establishments, with fewer departments to manage. However, the trend toward chain-affiliated hotels and motels should provide managers with opportunities for advancement into general manager positions and corporate administrative jobs. It appears that opportunities will be more limited for self-employed managers or owners of small lodging places. Job opportunities at outdoor recreation and RV parks should grow as RVs and driving vacations gain in popularity. Also, gaming services and gaming manager occupations should grow as more casino hotels are built.

Job turnover is relatively high in certain occupations in the hotel industry. To attract and retain workers, the industry is placing more emphasis on hiring and training. Nevertheless, many young people and others who are looking only for seasonal or part-time work, and not a career, take food service and clerical jobs that require little or no previous training. Therefore, job opportunities in this industry are plentiful for first-time jobseekers and people with limited skills.

In a message to readers of this book, the former president of the American Hotel Association, hotel industry leader Frank L. Andrews, stated:

> Regarding the future of the hotel business for the young men and women, naturally I am somewhat biased, having started in the industry as a very young man. I feel it offers all the advantages any other industry can offer. The success of the industry and of any other industry depends upon the aptitude of the individual, his willingness to work, and perseverance.

Income

It is difficult to try to estimate the salary one can expect in the hotel industry, since it includes workers of almost every occupation. Qualifications for each particular occupation vary and many factors must be taken into consideration, including education and experience. In addition, since many hotel workers depend largely on outside income, such as tips and service charges, the salary scale for their positions does not truly reflect their real earnings.

Salaries also vary according to the local wage scales for the various occupations and the size and location of the hotel. An added feature in estimating compensation is the fact that many hotel jobs include free meals and sometimes lodging and personal valet and laundry services as well. The latter are true especially of resort hotels, where all services such as laundry, valet, meals, and recreation facilities are provided for employees in addition to their rooms.

This book includes salary estimates for each occupation discussed. But remember that earnings vary greatly, and these estimates cannot be conclusive. You will find that some hotels provide meals and services for a person employed in a certain category, while another hotel will provide only a salary or wage for someone in the same occupation.

In general, earnings in the hotel industry range from a comparatively small weekly wage (augmented by tips, meals, lodging, and services, depending upon the hotel) to thousands of dollars paid out annually to top executives (see Chapters 4, 5, and 6 for specific occupational information).

2

Education and Training

Many of the nation's leading hotel executives started at the bottom and worked their way up the ladder of success. They began as assistant waiters, bellhops, room clerks, accountants, and pages. A good number of leading hotel executives have succeeded without benefit of special training. Years ago, when many of them first started out in the business, few schools or colleges offered courses in hotel management. In those days, hotel employees learned their trade only by apprenticeship or by working for a famous hotel executive and learning his or her system.

Today, however, hotel organizations are complex and require well-trained personnel. While many executives in the hotel industry came up the ladder without benefit of special educational or training courses, they grew up with hotels in a period when hotels themselves were growing. Today, although the hotel industry continues to expand and improve itself, its further maturity depends on properly trained personnel to perform the many jobs that make a hotel successful.

The skills and experience needed by workers in this industry is determined by the specific occupation. There are entry-level jobs that require little or no previous training. Basic tasks in these positions usually can be learned in a short time, and almost all workers in the hotel industry undergo on-the-job training, which usually is provided under the supervision of an experienced employee or manager. Some large chain operations have formal training sessions for new employees, and others have video training programs.

Hotel operations are becoming increasingly complex, with a greater emphasis being placed on specialized training. Community colleges, junior colleges, and some universities offer associate's, bachelor's, and graduate degree programs in hotel or restaurant management. Combined with technical institutes, vocational and trade schools, and other academic institutions, more than eight hundred educational facilities have programs leading to formal recognition in hotel or restaurant management. The U.S. Armed Forces also offer experience and training in food service. Many colleges throughout the United States and Canada offer hotel management programs that include instruction in hotel administration, accounting, economics, marketing, housekeeping, food service management and catering, and hotel maintenance engineering. Computer training also is an integral part of hotel management training, due to the widespread use of computers in reservations, billing, and housekeeping management. (See Appendix A for educational programs in hotel and hospitality management.)

General Education Studies

The best advice to anyone planning to enter the hotel industry is to prepare well for working in this field. A solid general education is the best foundation for any specialized courses that you pursue.

Expand your general studies as much as possible. A good general education will shape you into a well-rounded person and give you the ability to deal with diverse people and situations confidently and intelligently.

Your general studies should include learning other languages. Spanish is rapidly growing as the primary language of many business and leisure travelers, and it is the primary language of many hotel employees. French is an international language spoken by many foreign business travelers. For these reasons, both of these languages are very important in the hotel industry. It is also advisable to consider the ethnic makeup of any specific area in which you plan to work. If a city has a high Asian population, for example, it would be beneficial to learn the appropriate languages to communicate well with guests and fellow employees.

It is also useful to have a sound knowledge of geography. Since you are dealing with people who come from all sections of the nation and foreign countries, it is helpful to be able to speak knowledgeably about other locales. It is good business to know not only your guests, but also the cities and countries from which they come.

Successful hotel executives stress the importance of education for anyone considering a career in hotels, particularly in light of the changes the industry has undergone in recent years. Frank G. Wangeman, a former senior vice president of the Hilton Hotel Corporation and executive vice president of the Waldorf-Astoria Hotel, offers these thoughts about the importance of education:

> While the basic concepts of service and graciousness and honor to the guest remain the same as in great periods of culture centuries ago, the way of doing business [has changed] as business in the fashion of yesterday no longer stands up under modern demands; and even what is good enough today will be more than outmoded tomorrow. This, then, is the challenge of the hotel executive of

tomorrow. It offers . . . a great opportunity to come to the fore. The well-trained and aspiring youth will particularly find a calling in the hotel field—for youth, by its nature, is in tune with the times, and our business has to reflect the fashions of the times.

In the memory of many of us, the hotel business has grown from one of the small enterprises to . . . become "big business" . . . and it is in being in "big business" that I foresee the greatest challenges to the rising generation of hotel executives.

Although it is in your own best interest to earn a college degree to build a good background for your specialized hotel training, it is not a necessity. If circumstances prevent you from completing your education, there are still many opportunities for you to enter the hotel industry and advance up the ladder while learning the business from the inside. A large hotel employs a broad cross section of workers in many occupations. For this reason, it is impossible to set up rigid educational requirements for entrance into the field, since necessary training varies with each particular profession. When you consider that the occupations related to the hotel industry include carpentry, plumbing, electrical work, and other trades, you can understand the variation possible in educational requirements and preparation.

As previously mentioned, there are many jobs in the hotel industry for which no special education or training is required. These are mostly unskilled and lower-paying positions; workers in these positions are generally trained by hotel management or department heads. These jobs might include waiter, maid, clerk, page, housekeeper, porter, or elevator operator.

It is possible, however, for employees to be promoted from these lower-level jobs to positions of greater responsibility and higher pay. The best way to pursue promotion is to continue your education after hours. If possible, enroll in special courses in hotel training, such as those often offered by community colleges as part of adult education programs. If you intend to pursue a career in the hotel industry, education and completion of special hotel training courses is almost a necessity. Large hotels and hotel chains give preference to educated employees. They particularly seek employees who have completed special hotel training courses given by recognized schools and colleges. Educated and trained personnel make better hotel employees, and they will become the executives and hotel industry leaders of tomorrow.

Computer training is also an integral part of hotel management. Every large hotel and establishment that is part of a chain uses computers for reservations, housekeeping management, and billing. Even small bed-and-breakfast inns use computers to manage their operations.

A further observation from former hotel executive Frank Wangeman stresses the importance of education:

> We must never forget that the basic skills in innkeeping will bring us success or failure; however, these basic skills, as essential as they are, will not serve as the future hotel executive's foundation unless they are coupled with modern business methods.
>
> Looking back at the great leaders in our business over the last half century, whether it was Caesar Ritz, E. M. Statler, Lucious Boomer, Conrad Hilton, or others, each and every one was ahead of his time. The future leaders of our business will, of course, also be ahead of their time, which means that they will have to pioneer in fields of scientific and business knowledge that were unheard of in the days of our great predecessors.
>
> I can therefore urge my young friends in the hotel business to equip themselves with the best possible all-around education. This education will bring rewards well beyond their fond expectations; for what is there more thrilling than to be an integral, vibrant part of a great business that encompasses practically each and every

phase of human life, and that is bound to grow and further develop with the progress in the various fields of transportation?

Early Preparation

Contact the school or college of your choice as early as possible to be properly prepared to meet the entrance requirements. You can find out if your preparation is along the proper lines only by contacting the individual schools and colleges and ascertaining their requirements.

The best way to gather detailed information about courses of study offered, entrance prerequisites, registration, tuition fees, and other requirements is to contact the school directly. An Internet search will lead you to the websites of any schools in which you are interested; there you can research the pertinent information you need to make an informed decision. You can also request a school catalog at most websites.

Probably the most useful source of educational information on programs nationwide is the *College Blue Book*. This five-volume set is particularly useful to those seeking highly specialized programs. The volume entitled *Occupational Education* includes a list of available programs of study in technical schools and community colleges, organized alphabetically by state or by subject area. Another volume, *Degrees Offered by College and Subject*, includes degree programs offered by two-year colleges, four-year colleges, and universities. Other volumes offer narrative descriptions of schools, costs, accreditation, enrollment figures, scholarships, fellowships, grants, loans, and a lot of other information.

The *College Blue Book* can be found in the reference section of the library along with many other educational resources. Most college and university libraries also carry a variety of college catalogs, enabling one to compare the curricula of different schools offering the degree or program of interest.

Another useful source of information is Peterson's online guide (www.petersons.com). This website offers a searchable database of two- and four-year colleges, graduate schools, career programs, and study abroad, among other options. Information is available on test preparation, financial aid, admissions essays, and résumé writing. Peterson's also offers books and materials for sale on various educational and career topics.

The American Hotel and Lodging Association (AH&LA) offers education and training materials through its Educational Institute (EI). See Chapter 3 for more information about the AH&LA.

Apprenticeship and Training

Hotels offer greater opportunities for beginners to apprentice and train than many other industries. In addition, few other industries can offer the added convenience of work schedules that can be coordinated with school hours. The three-shift system used by many hotels may make it easier for students to work after school hours in apprentice jobs.

The three common hotel shifts are 7:30 A.M. to 3:30 P.M., 3:30 to 11:30 P.M., and 11:30 P.M. to 7:30 A.M. In some hotels this timing has been adjusted to the even hours, 8:00 A.M., 4:00 P.M., and midnight. The second shift works well for many student trainees. On-the-job training is an important part of many courses in hotel work, since it supplements classroom instruction with hands-on experience.

For students who want to enter the hotel industry without attending a special hotel training school or taking hotel courses, it is a good idea to apply for a part-time job at a hotel. Opportunities as bellhop, elevator operator, page, key clerk, mail clerk, information clerk, file clerk, office helper, chef's helper, kitchen helper, front office assistant, and waiterperson are often filled by part-time employees. Many students put themselves through high school, college, and hotel training courses by taking part-time or full-time jobs during the after-school hours in hotels.

A part-time job is an excellent way to discover whether you really like the hotel business. It is a comparatively easy way to learn about the industry and decide if you like it well enough to continue your studies in hotel administration. On-the-job training is highly valued, and in hotel training courses, special credits are given for this work. On-the-job training or apprenticeship can substitute partly for outside studies until such time as you are able to complete a hotel training course.

The Educational Institute of the American Hotel and Lodging Association offers training programs designed to accommodate beginners from different areas. EI's Lodging Management Program (LMP) provides eleventh- and twelfth-grade students with the classroom learning and hands-on work experiences needed to work in the various areas of the hotel industry. More than 450 high schools in forty-five states offer the LMP, which teaches management principles and leads to a professional certification called the Certified Rooms Division Specialist. Many colleges and universities grant participants credit toward a postsecondary degree in hotel management.

The Skills, Tasks, and Results Training Program (START) is a one-year or 180-classroom-hour curriculum that gives students the real-world knowledge and skills needed for a long-term career in the lodging industry. This program is designed for such targeted groups as at-risk youth, welfare-to-work, and dislocated workers. Ninth- and tenth-grade students can also use it as preparation for the LMP program.

The AH&LA also offers professional certification in many areas of hospitality management. Certification is available for line-level positions as well as departmental and executive positions. Complete information about all AH&LA programs is available at the organization's website, http://ahla.com.

If you think you would like to enter the hotel business; if you feel yourself qualified to enter it; if you are ambitious, energetic, and not afraid of hard work; if you are tolerant, understanding, and like all kinds of people from all walks of life, then let nothing stand in your way.

Barron Hilton, president and chief executive officer of the Hilton Hotels Corporation, offers his view of the importance of education for a career in the hotel industry:

> An adequate education is fundamental to one's success in our industry, as it is to one's success in any industry of American business. For those desiring specialized educational training for our industry, many of our nation's largest universities offer outstanding hotel and restaurant management schools. However, I think it well to point out that even such specialized training does not guarantee employment in our industry, but it does highly qualify one to seek such an opportunity. For those having the patience and willingness to invest a period of employment equivalent to that which they have invested in an education, to learn the practical application of their training, for learning the particular operation of companies to join, and to demonstrate their desire to stand apart in effort and creativity, their success is a foregone conclusion.

Career Opportunities

Given the many different types of lodging establishments that exist and the variety of services they provide, the hotel industry offers a multitude of career opportunities. Jobs exist for workers with a wide range of education, training, and work experience, in full-time, part-time, and even seasonal employment.

Hotel careers can be divided into these major categories:

- **Front office staff**—Responsible for direct personal contact with guests and handling reservations, special needs, check-in, and checkout
- **Service staff**—Responsible for greeting guests, handling baggage, and assisting with travel plans
- **Accounting**—Responsible for tracking financial information critical to the operations of any business
- **Food service**—Responsible for making every meal a pleasant and enjoyable experience
- **Food preparation**—Responsible for ensuring safe and proper food preparation
- **Housekeeping**—Responsible for maintaining a neat and clean home for visitors
- **Sales**—Responsible for promotions; handling special arrangements for groups such as meetings, banquets, and conventions; and all special events such as weddings
- **Other departments and services**—Responsible for security, safety, fire protection, room service, laundry, dry cleaning, and so forth

An executive officer of the American Hotel and Lodging Association offers this perspective on careers in the industry:

A career in the lodging industry offers excellent opportunities for advancement. Lack of experience or education is not a barrier to employment in the lodging industry—it only determines where your career begins. Once you have entered the field, the pace at which you move upward largely depends on your willingness to work hard, the desire to do a good job, your level of enthusiasm, and eagerness to advance. On-the-job training programs are plentiful, and excellent courses are available through the Educational Institute of the American Hotel and [Lodging] Association. Fees for vocational training courses are often reimbursed by your employer.

Because of the size and scope of the lodging industry, there is something for everyone who wants to work in this field. It's a fast-paced growth industry that offers new jobs each year, with excellent job security and opportunities for advancement. Further, you can travel and select where you want to work, the hours, and even the season, if you wish!

Salaries compare favorably with other retail trades, plus there are many extra benefits not reflected in salary. For example, in many cases, at least one meal is furnished, excellent benefit plans are available, and often bonus programs can earn individuals up to 30 percent of their base salary.

Personal Attributes

The most important personal trait necessary for success in the hotel industry is the ability to get along with all kinds of people under all kinds of conditions. The people you must deal with in this industry, guests and employees alike, vary widely in terms of education, personal experience, intelligence, business background, nationality, and personal characteristics.

You should ask yourself one important question: Do you like all people well enough to overlook their idiosyncrasies? If you think you do, then this is the field for you. To succeed in the hotel industry, you must be broadminded, tolerant, understanding, and humane. It is important to keep in mind that you will regularly be dealing with many different temperaments in various situations.

Any person contemplating a career in the hotel industry should be neat, have a flair for detail, and be willing to be of service to others. This last requirement is not a catchall phrase; it embodies the ability to listen attentively, have a ready smile, and maintain a reserved manner. Therefore, anyone with an uncontrollable temper or an inbred shyness must try to overcome these defects to have a successful career in the hotel industry. To those who feel qualified to make a career out of the hotel business, the pleasant surroundings, the opportunity to meet new people, and the gratification derived from rendering service are but a few of the rewards of a job well done.

One of the most successful hotel operators in the industry is Preston R. Tisch, cochairman of Loews Hotels. Tisch and his brother, Laurence A. Tisch, who was chairman of the board and chief executive officer of Loews Corporation, created one of this nation's leading hotel chains. Preston Tisch comments on qualities that contribute to success in the hotel field:

> The good hotel [employee], whether a general manager or bell-hop, has to like people to be successful. For after all, it is people with whom you will be dealing—not machines or cardboard cartons. I will pay more for the ability to handle people than for any other quality or trait. By people I mean not only the guests but the other employees in the hotel. Generally, the good host is born with this ability. But, to a certain extent, it can be acquired, and it must be acquired if one is to get ahead in hotels.
>
> Second, I would list attention to detail. Very often I find that the most vehement complaints from patrons are due to seemingly insignificant omissions on the part of staff members. A restaurant guest will wait uncomplainingly in line to get a table at a busy restaurant, but will go completely berserk over a dirty water glass or an overly hard dinner roll. He will accept a smaller room than the one he reserved, but will blow his top because a washcloth is

missing from the bath. The waiter or the housekeeper who is lax in the little things automatically puts the entire hotel in a bad light. Some guests will become so wrought up over minor details that they will never return.

Third, every hotel employee must bear in mind the old axiom that the "customer is always right," even if he is entirely wrong. To attempt to defend yourself against an unjust attack is only natural; nevertheless, you must bear in mind that the complainant has paid good money in your establishment, and, in his own mind, there is nobody more important than he. You can prove he is wrong, but in doing so you are bound to lose him and the friends he might otherwise recommend. The smart hotelier will immediately disarm the guest by agreeing with him and offering to make things right without delay. Of course, there are exceptions to this rule, and those are the ones in which some heavy financial outlay is involved by way of restitution.

Fourth, hotel people who want to make progress in their field should give a little more than the job requires. It is the self-starter, the one who develops new ideas on her or his own initiative, who will amount to something in the long [run]. This is the person we are constantly looking for at Loews Hotels.

3

The Job Search

Many schools and colleges offer employment assistance for students. In some cases, the schools have arrangements with certain hotels and hotel chains for the placement of graduates. If this is not the case, you will need to conduct your own employment search. This will also be true for beginners who seek employment but have no formal hotel training.

Large hotels and hotel chains have human resources departments that are responsible for hiring new employees. Write, telephone, e-mail, or visit in person the office of the employment director (or assistant manager or personnel director) of those hotels or chains with which you wish to seek employment. Your goal will be not only to register for employment, but also to get yourself interviewed by the person in charge. If an opening exists, you must "sell" yourself as you would to get any job. Many chains list job openings on their websites.

Where there are no openings, request information concerning other hotels or cities where possible openings may exist for you based on your experience, education, or background. Hotel people, especially those in the human resources departments, often know of such openings. If you have made a good impression, chances are that you may receive information concerning other opportunities.

In large hotels, it may also be helpful to communicate directly with the heads of those departments for which you might qualify. Departmental heads often hire and fire their own employees. If you can sell your personality and ability to the manager or executive head of the organization, he or she may wish to hire you as a trainee. Many managers are eager to find promising personnel for consideration as future executives, and they have the authority to add to the payroll.

The American Hotel and Lodging Association

There are hotel associations in almost every state. One of the tasks they usually perform for members is to act as a clearinghouse for personnel. They often send out regular lists of available people to member hotels. Communicate with your state associations and with associations in other states where you might wish to work. While permanent headquarters for these associations are maintained in some states, in most states the headquarters change each year with the election of new officers. For the correct address of the hotel association in your state, communicate with any hotel in your community. (See Appendix B for a select list of professional associations.)

The American Hotel and Lodging Association (AH&LA), located in Washington, DC, represents practically all leading hotels and motels in the United States and has more than ten thousand property members nationwide. The AH&LA offers many services to its members, such as legal, accounting, employee relations advice, and other helpful information. The association is also a clearing center for specialized requests. The AH&LA website (http://ahla.com) offers a wealth of information about the industry, and provides links to the existing state associations.

The AH&LA offers student membership, too. One of the most valuable benefits of student membership is access to the AH&LA Career Center, which includes the largest online database of job openings in the lodging industry. The association also has an Educational Institute (EI), through which it offers education and training materials to all levels of workers in the hospitality industry. The EI offers certification in every specialty of the industry, as well as the highest credentials, Certified Hotel Administrator (CHA) and Certified Lodging Manager (CLM). The Educational Institute can be visited at www.ei-ahla.org.

Interviewing

It is important to remember that hotel work is service work, and that a hotel's reputation depends on the quality of service it offers to guests. In a hotel, the personnel must always be polite, speak correctly, and use good manners. A neat and clean appearance is a must for employees who provide any type of service to guests.

Keep these points in mind when you apply for a position in a hotel. If you consider the interviewer's priorities, you should be able to act accordingly during an interview. You will be judged on your intelligence, your appearance, your manners, and your willingness to learn. It is important to remember that the interviewer is looking for a levelheaded, self-controlled, flexible person, for someone who can adapt to changing situations and get along with all different kinds of people.

Above all, when you apply for a position in the hotel field, remember your appearance. One of the most important requirements in the hotel business is good appearance. Hotel people, by the very nature of their work, are required to be well groomed at all times. You cannot expect to make a good impression when interviewing for a hotel job unless you are neat, clean, and appropriately dressed. Good grooming makes sense.

Advancement

The history of the hotel industry shows that the path to success is wide open for ambitious, intelligent, energetic people. Hotel policy usually gives preference on job openings to current employees who are enthusiastic and efficient workers. Many of today's top hotel executives have come up through the ranks, some starting as far down the ladder as assistant waiters, bellhops, and clerks. Tomorrow's hotel leaders may be an assistant waiter in San Francisco, a room clerk in Dallas, an accountant in Philadelphia. Even if they never become top executives, beginners are often promoted to more responsible positions. Housekeepers often start as maids, chefs as apprentices, restaurant managers as assistant waiters.

The length of time between promotions in the hotel industry varies. There is no set schedule or plan of advancement in most hotels. The only organizations where regular promotions are given are those conducting executive-training or exchange programs. In the former, someone being groomed for executive work will be rotated into different hotel departments to become familiar with the operations of the hotel. In an exchange program, hotels exchange department or subdepartment heads with one another to share ideas and learn from each other's operations.

In general, there is greater turnover in a large hotel than in a small hotel. Accordingly, swifter advancement is possible in large hotels because openings occur more often, and changes are made to fill vacancies. The law of averages will operate more to your advantage in an organization with many employees, as management must replace workers who retire, resign, or transfer to other positions.

Management in most small hotels is identical with ownership. This limits your future prospects unless you can raise enough capital to buy or become a partner in a hotel. Most large hotels, by their size alone, represent huge investments and are owned by corporations representing the financial interests of banks, insurance companies, or joint stock companies. Some hotels have been financed by public stock issues. Since the large hotels are generally controlled or managed but seldom owned completely, their corporate structure creates opportunities that would not exist in a privately owned enterprise. Corporations offer greater opportunities for advancement and often make top posts available to rank outsiders.

Uppermost positions in the hotel industry are attained only after many years of managerial and executive experience in the industry. The larger the hotel, the more experience is required. There is a great difference between managing a medium-sized hotel and operating a huge establishment of a thousand or more rooms with many public and dining halls. You can get to one of the top hotels' posts only after you have had considerable experience in larger hotels.

Advancement in the hotel industry is unique and quite peculiar. Comparatively rapid, it does not follow a regular pattern, and it may be indirect. In most industries, employees advance or receive increases only after they have spent long periods of time in each position they hold. And in private industry, advancement is more commonly indicated by salary increases rather than a change in position. A driller in the oil industry keeps receiving pay increases, but no one would think of promoting the driller to assistant credit manager. A post office delivery person receives automatic pay increases, but no postmaster would promote the delivery person to a higher position as engraver in the Treasury Department.

In the hotel industry, however, employees who merit advancement step into positions higher up in rank and salary. But this step up may lead the employee into an entirely different department. The advancement may even mean a move to another hotel, sometimes in a different city or country. For this reason, it is always beneficial to take outside training courses. Contact department heads in the hotel and ask to be considered for various openings. Many opportunities exist; it is up to you to take them.

Alan S. Jeffrey, previous director of the American Hotel and Lodging Association Educational Institute, writes that the hotel and motel field offers a future in one of the most exciting industries in the world today:

> If you are seeking an exciting future, enjoy meeting and working with people in a growing industry with good pay, job security, and the opportunity to travel and live in different places, you may be just the person who should seek a career in the lodging industry.
>
> There is some excitement about the hospitality business that is like none other. It is interesting, challenging, and rewarding. However, there are times when it is also frustrating. It is fast moving and hectic. Hotels and motels operate twenty-four hours a day, seven days a week, catering to the needs of people on the move. . . .
>
> Providing away-from-home lodging and meals is one of the largest and fastest-growing industries in the country today. The need for qualified employees is growing just as fast as the industry. Since more people travel today than ever before, and because of the increasing amount of leisure time most Americans enjoy, hotels and motels continue to be built. This means increased job opportunities.

4

THE FRONT OF THE HOUSE: GUEST SERVICES

IN GENERAL, THE *front of the house* refers to those departments whose employees interact directly with hotel guests. The services performed by these departments impact every guest in some way. Because management has overall responsibility for these areas, front of the house also includes management departments. Service, front office, accounting, credit, security, human resources, banquet, advertising, public relations, sales, resident management, executive management, and all subdivisions of these departments make up the front of the house. While there are important positions in the back of the house, most top positions and all executive posts lie in the front.

Given the large number of departments that comprise the front of the house, the topic is divided into two chapters. This chapter will cover the departments that deal directly with hotel guests: service, front office, security, and banquet and catering. Chapter 5 will cover accounting, purchasing, central files, human resources, public relations and advertising, sales, and other management positions.

Whether your hotel career begins in the front or back of the house (see Chapter 6) depends on your likes and dislikes, your educational and training background, and your ability and skill in the various professions. But regardless of which side you choose to enter, the opportunities are equal. Only the paths along which you rise will be different.

Even if you start in the front and proceed up the ladder, you will find that knowledge of back-of-the-house operations is most important. Somewhere along your advance in the hotel business, you will need to study, if not actually practice, back-of-the-house duties and operations. Take courses in food operations, housekeeping, purchasing, and other back-of-the-house departments. Try to work in the various departments, if possible. Round out your hotel experience and training with an all-around background in both front- and back-of-the-house operations.

Service Department

The service department of most hotels offers beginners in the industry wonderful opportunities for starting their careers. In addition, they are an excellent means for advancement because service department jobs often are stepping-stones to the top of the ladder.

A hotel's entire function is to provide service. However, certain duties that deal with personal service provided for guests entering or leaving the hotel are grouped together and performed by a separate department set up for that purpose. This department is called the service department, and the head of the department is the guest service manager. Other titles for this position include superintendent of service, assistant manager in charge of service, or chief of service. Working under the guest service manager are bellhops, door attendants, the concierge, elevator operators, porters, and checking room attendants. The duties of baggage and washroom attendants and pages are sometimes included in this department as well.

Guest Service Manager

The members of the service department provide guests with their first impressions of a hotel. The treatment given guests by the door attendant, the bellhop who takes their luggage, and the elevator operator influences guests' opinions of the hotel. Therefore, the position of guest service manager is an important one, and it also offers fringe benefits (such as free meals) and good opportunity for advancement.

The guest service manager is responsible for hiring, instructing, disciplining, and discharging employees in the department. The efficiency of service employees will depend to a large extent upon the efficiency of this manager's instruction methods, his or her own personal hotel experience and background, and the type of personnel he or she employs.

The manager must ensure that all jobs that fall under his or her purview are done properly. Door attendants must be prompt in opening doors of automobiles, ready to help guests in and out of vehicles, and willing to carry baggage from curb to door where bellhops will pick it up. Elevators must be operated safely and on the best possible schedule. The operators must be neat and clean, must call off the floors promptly, and must be polite in their dealings with guests. Self-service elevators must be watched and regulated. Package room attendants must ensure the safe delivery of packages to guests. Bellhops must be alert and intelligent and must respond quickly to the wishes of guests. They must be well trained in hotel procedure, such as hanging clothes in closets, opening windows, checking bathroom supplies and facilities, and checking rooms for completion of proper maid service.

Most guest service managers have risen to their posts after years of experience, in some cases as many as ten years. Occasionally, front office clerks are promoted to this position. The jobs of bell captain and head baggage porter are other possible starting points for the manager's position. However, the office of guest service manager is not necessarily a last stop. It is often a stepping-stone job, and many managers have advanced to higher positions in the same or other hotels.

Bell Captains and Bellhops

Found in most medium-sized and all large hotels, the position of bell captain is the second-ranking job in the service department. After guest service manager, it is the job most sought after in this department. And in some of the larger hotels, people prefer this post to that of manager because of its financial and other advantages.

Bell captains attain their posts only after years of experience, usually as a bellhop. Definitely a stepping-stone position in the hotel organization, the job of bell captain offers opportunities for operational experience.

It is the duty of the bell captain to keep time records of all bellhops, to instruct all new employees, to arrange the immediate dispatch of bellhops on guest calls, to rate the bellhops fairly so that all share evenly in the tips, and to assign bellhops efficiently so that all incoming guests are met and all guests' requests are seen to. The bell captain is also responsible for interviewing new job applicants, investigating and responding to guests' complaints relating to the work of the department, and deciding whether unusual guest requests should be filled. An efficient bell captain can make the difference between good and bad service for hotel guests.

The bell captain's staff includes bellhops and sometimes pages. Bellhops perform a multitude of tasks. They are charged with ushering incoming guests to their rooms and carrying their baggage. Bellhops sometimes help set up rooms and bring ice water, food, or other items requested by guests. Bellhops occasionally perform special duties like delivering letters or packages (with the special permission of the bell captain), picking up theater tickets, making travel arrangements, and other personal service chores.

Bellhops must be diplomats, able to judge people and know how to make them feel comfortable and at home in their hotel rooms. They must be prepared to provide local information and answer questions about the hotel and its surrounding area. As the first connecting link between the guest and the hotel, the impression they create is important.

Positions as bellhops are secured by applying to the human resources department or bell captain. Some hotels select their bellhops from the ranks of elevator operators or starters, while others employ bellhops who have had experience elsewhere. But the methods of employment differ depending on the individual hotel's hiring policies. Some hotels employ bellhops who have had no experience at all. In communities where courses in bellhop training are given by schools, hotels, or hotel associations, local hotels may require their bellhops to attend the courses either before or during employment.

There are many advancement opportunities for bellhops. The next step is promotion to bell captain, then guest service manager, and then up to the various other managerial posts. Bellhops may sometimes move to other hotels where better opportunities exist.

Very good opportunities for entering the ranks of bellhops exist in resort hotels, where new crews are hired every season or where large turnovers are common. After gaining experience there, one can transfer to a commercial hotel. Many bellhops start as elevator operators or housekeepers and work their way up. The length of time it takes to advance depends on the size of the hotel's staff and the rate of turnover.

Bellhops usually work eight hours a day for six days a week. In large hotels, the three-shift system is employed to provide twenty-four-hour service. In this case, beginners are often given the night shift.

Head Baggage Porters

Most large hotels employ a head baggage porter in addition to the bell captain. Although the previously listed duties of the baggage porter are the same as those of the bell captain and bellhops, in larger establishments this work is handled exclusively by baggage porters. The head baggage porter must keep time records of all employees in the department; interview, instruct, discipline, and discharge employees; rotate the staff on calls equitably; and, in general, perform the same supervisory function as the bell captain.

Setting up rooms, supplying travel information, buying transportation tickets, arranging shipment of express articles, and handling baggage and suitcases for departing guests are the exclusive duties of the baggage porter in larger hotels. For this reason, this position is also commonly referred to as the transportation clerk, whose office may be called the transportation desk.

Baggage porters are generally appointed from the elevator operating staff, housekeeping ranks, or other service departments of the hotel. Occasionally, a hotel will appoint a baggage porter who has had no outside experience. People with experience at other hotels are also considered.

Baggage porters aspire to be head baggage porter. Most porters reach this position only after several years of experience. The next step up the ladder is appointment as guest service manager. However, this promotion more often goes to the bell captain than to the head baggage porter. From guest service manager, the path leads to front office or managerial positions.

The working hours and conditions of employment for baggage porters are usually the same as those for bellhops.

Other Service Department Functions

Service departments of hotels differ depending on the size of the hotel and staff and the operation policy of the hotel's management. Departmental setups will vary from hotel to hotel.

Accordingly, some hotels offer additional opportunities for employment in the service department. These positions include door attendant, checking attendant, porter, page, secretary to the guest service manager, lobby attendant, restroom attendant, shoeshine attendant, and others. For further information, apply to the human resources department or guest service manager for details of other jobs in a specific hotel.

Hours and Earnings

With the exception of the head of this department, hours of work in the service departments of most hotels are based on the three-shift system. Hours will vary depending on the size of the hotel and nature of its operation, and this three-shift system might not then apply. In general, however, employees in this department work about eight hours a day, five or six days a week.

Pay also varies depending on the size and location of the hotel. Earnings in hotel service positions are generally lower than they are in other industries, with many workers earning the federal minimum wage of $5.15 per hour. However, bellhops and porters make more money in larger hotels or resort hotels where more services are demanded. In these settings, their earnings may run as high as $500 weekly and more, including tips.

The average nationwide salary of guest service managers in 2002 was $34,134. Larger hotels offer higher salaries than do smaller establishments, and geographic location is also a factor in determining pay rate. Bell captains and head baggage porters average about the same income as guest service managers. Because the head baggage porter often arranges for transportation services, this person's income can sometimes be greater just by virtue of large tips received on these transactions.

Because most, though not all, earnings in this department are augmented by tips and side money, one cannot consider the average wage as the complete remuneration. In general, earnings of service department employees run much higher than their base average wage scales would indicate. Earnings here may vary from city to city and hotel to hotel. As indication of the potential earning capacity in these service jobs, people who have been bellhops or baggage porters for many years in some of the larger hotels have refused promotions many times, preferring their current positions.

Hotel Front Office

The entire responsibility for processing reservations, registering guests, and keeping records of room vacancies is in the hands of the hotel's front office. The front office must conduct these functions efficiently so that the front office manager always has enough information to make firm reservations for guests without over-booking hotel facilities. In addition, the front office performs all tasks related to registering and keeping track of guests, including providing keys and mail service.

Front Office Manager

One of the most important positions in the hotel is the front office manager. This person is charged with the responsibility of esti-mating the volume of future reservations, preparing for busy sea-sons, organizing all departmental functions so that they operate efficiently, and maintaining a close check at all times on occupied and available rooms and firm reservations. The front office man-ager must keep all departments well balanced and in coordination with one another.

Promotion to this position is generally made from front office clerks, assistant managers on the floor, credit office personnel, or other workers. Occasionally hotels will hire front office managers from outside the hotel. From front office manager, the next step up is toward a management executive post.

Working under the front office manager are room and reserva-tion clerks; key, mail, and information clerks; floor clerks (also known as assistant managers on the floor); hospitality department workers and secretaries; and filing clerks, word processors, and other clerical workers.

Front office managers, because of the importance of their work and the large number of employees they supervise, must have exten-sive hotel experience, ability, and mature judgment. Their author-ity over rooms is second only to that of the director of sales and the manager.

Clerks

A front office clerk generally has at least a high school education and has completed some courses in hotel training either before or during employment. Although many positions in the front office do not require higher education or special preliminary training, the opportunities offered in the department induce many front office employees to enhance their job experience with hotel training courses. This is especially true with front office clerks, as their job is considered a stepping-stone for managerial positions.

Front office clerks perform various duties. In smaller hotels, the front office clerk, or manager, may perform all front office duties. In larger hotels, the work is departmentalized. The front office clerks consist of room clerks, who sell rooms and follow through on all functions of guest registration; reservation clerks, who acknowledge and make reservations by phone, letter, fax, or e-mail; and various other subdivisions, depending on the size of the hotel and its staff.

In general, front office duties include the mechanical processing of reservations, sale and registration of rooms, furnishing guest keys or key cards, and handling complaints about rooms or other accommodations. Front office clerks also receive and forward mail, give information about guests registered or expected (where permitted), and provide local information concerning room rates and times of departure.

While front office clerks are sometimes employed directly from outside applicants, it is general hotel practice to fill these openings with other staff employees, such as bellhops, credit workers, clerical employees, or other personnel. For the more responsible jobs in this department, people with similar experience at other hotels are often hired.

Since front office clerk is a possible stepping-stone to a managerial position, a college degree is recommended for success. If you cannot continue your general education, you should definitely complete special courses in hotel training given by the schools and colleges listed in Appendix A. You can complete special hotel training courses while you are employed, if necessary. The three-shift system usually prevails in the front office. The shift employing the fewest workers is the night shift, since most new guests arrive during the daylight hours, or before midnight at the latest.

In small hotels, the owner-manager may handle the duties of the front office with or without an assistant. There is more opportunity for advancement and for obtaining knowledge in a large hotel than in a small one. The larger hotel, because of its size and scope of operations, offers many more chances to perform hotel duties.

Assistant Managers

In larger hotels, the front office staff includes assistant managers. They are on duty "on the floor" (the lobby floor), acting as troubleshooters and ambassadors of good will for the improvement of guest relations.

Representing the hotel's management, assistant managers handle complaints from guests and assist in straightening out problems and any emergencies that may occur. Regular duties include helping guests make reservations at hotels in other cities, changing guests' rooms as requested, notifying the security department of disorderly or undesirable individuals spotted throughout the hotel, assisting with guest registration at rush check-in hours, and helping to register special guests quickly or quietly when requested. Assistant managers see that operations at the front office, in the lobby, and throughout the hotel are functioning properly and that the guests are satisfied.

Although assistant managers are authorized to assume managerial status in emergencies and other situations, they are responsible to the front office manager, and the major part of their duties concerns front office operations. In addition to expediting guest arrivals and registrations, assistant managers on the floor also relieve the manager and executive assistants of the many minor problems that occur daily in hotel operation.

Members of the front office staff are usually appointed assistant manager. Front office clerks, chief room clerks, and others are next in line for the position.

Assistant managers work the same hours as the rest of the front office. Since they are a step higher on the ladder of front office operations, the education and training requirements are the same or greater than those for front office clerks.

Mail and Information

The mail and information department offers excellent opportunities for beginners in the hotel industry. In smaller hotels front office clerks assume the duties of this department; in larger hotels this work is more specialized. Duties include handling incoming and outgoing guest mail, supplying information concerning guests' room numbers, clearing such room information for the telephone department and other hotel departments, maintaining guest-room key racks, and furnishing guests with room keys or key cards.

Mail and information is a desirable department in which to begin a hotel career. Many newcomers to the field are employed in this phase of work, and the department offers good opportunities for advancement. Educational requirements are essentially the same as those for front office clerks. The work here is not necessarily skilled, and the head of the department usually provides any required training. However, the better your education and training, the better background you will have for advancement.

As hours here are based on the same three-shift system used by the rest of front office employees, openings are possible for after-school work. Applicants with no previous experience can find jobs. Occasionally, personnel from other departments are employed at this desk when they are being considered for further promotions.

Hospitality Department/Concierge

Most large commercial and resort hotels have hospitality departments. In smaller hotels, room clerks, assistant managers, bellhops, or other employees who come in contact with guests carry out the duties of this department.

The role of the concierge has grown in importance in recent years. A long-standing European custom, the concierge position has immigrated to the United States and is fairly common in most major and luxury hotels. The concierge and superintendent of service positions may be the same in some instances, but generally the concierge is a sole entity, similar in many ways to the old hospitality desk that once existed in most hotel lobbies. The concierge will arrange special requests, such as assisting guests in obtaining theater tickets or securing reservations at popular restaurants. In hotels dealing with foreign visitors, the concierge will speak more than one language.

Sometimes the function of hospitality personnel is to act as hosts for guests of the hotel. The duties include providing guests with information about local points of interest; keeping daily listings of local motion picture and theatrical entertainment; providing special services, such as babysitters, companions, and personal maid service; obtaining concert and event tickets for guests; arranging sightseeing tours; and helping guests make reservations at hotels in other cities.

An assistant manager (front office) on duty typically has supervision of the hospitality staff. The usual hours of work are during the two daytime shifts of the three-shift system. As in most hotel jobs, a position in the hospitality department can lead to other opportunities, such as sales, front desk, and other departments.

For work here, one should be well informed about local points of interest, have good knowledge of nearby highways and transportation routes, keep abreast of play and motion picture reviews, and, in general, be in touch with all local social, church, theatrical, and other such events. Knowledge of other languages is also helpful, particularly in hotels with a large international clientele or those in areas with a high concentration of a specific ethnic group.

Hours and Earnings

As previously stated, most front office employees work on the three-shift system. It is not uncommon for beginners to start on the night shift and advance to one of the day shifts with experience. In some cases, workers rotate among the three shifts.

The front office may offer greater opportunity for promotion than any other department of the hotel. The hotel business is primarily one of selling rooms, food, and liquor. Here in the front office, you are face-to-face with guests, their problems, their complaints, and their likes and dislikes. You can watch the hotel as its rooms empty and fill on charts and computer screens before you. Many of today's hotel executives started out in front office positions.

Average front office earnings vary, depending upon the size of the hotel, the number of employees, and the size of the city. Typical salaries for front office clerks averaged $8.32 per hour in 2002 for an eight-hour day and a five- to six-day week. Earnings of apprentices, and mail and information, and key and other clerks may start lower and vary, depending upon locations.

The salary of the front office manager is well above the departmental average, but earnings vary greatly in this department. In some hotels, certain front office jobs include meals as part of the remuneration. In 2002, assistant front office managers averaged $37,721 annually; front office managers averaged $39,496. The average salary of a concierge was $38,340.

Security Department

Hotel security departments range from a solitary employee in some small hotels to as many as twenty or more people in large establishments. The primary concern of house officers and patrol personnel is the protection of hotel guests and their property

In most large hotels, the security staff operates under the supervision of a director of security (or chief house officer) to safeguard hotel guests and property against theft or other crimes. Members of the department are stationed in public rooms, in the lobby, on banquet floors, and on the guest floors. House officers are also trained to help guests in distress, prevent disturbances in any part of the hotel, accompany cashiers, prevent annoyance of guests, and take charge in case of emergencies.

In addition to house officers, the security departments of large hotels also include uniformed patrol personnel. These guards regularly tour all guest floors, service floors, and public rooms. In many hotels, they punch time clocks at stations along their tour. They inspect the premises continually to see that things are in order. Other patrol personnel are assigned to the receiving entrance to prevent loss of merchandise. They are also assigned to patrol work at conventions, banquets, and when large crowds are in any of the public rooms.

The security department may also house the lost and found section where all articles left in rooms by departing guests, or found elsewhere in the hotel, are kept for return to their owners. In some hotels, the housekeeping department handles this function. Here, too, reports of losses are made to house officers.

There are not any specific educational requirements for unarmed guards. For armed guards, employers usually prefer individuals who are high school graduates or hold an equivalent certification. For positions as armed guards, employers often seek people who have had responsible experience in other occupations. Many are former police officers.

Guards who carry weapons must be licensed by the appropriate government authority, and they have more stringent background checks and entry requirements than do unarmed guards because of greater insurance liability risks. Most establishments that employ security guards use rigorous hiring and screening programs consisting of background, criminal record, and fingerprint checks. Applicants are expected to have good character references, no serious police record, and good health. They should be mentally alert, emotionally stable, and physically fit to cope with emergencies. Guards who have frequent contact with the public should also be able to communicate well.

Hours and Earnings

Since security is a twenty-four-hour operation, the three-shift system is generally employed by members of the department. In 2002, median annual earnings of hotel guards were $21,390. In general, earnings depend on the size and location of the hotel, number of hours worked, and the employee's experience. The average earnings of directors of security were $44,801. Meals are sometimes furnished to the manager or other security personnel.

Promotions are possible within the security department and also to other departments such as front office, credit, and management. The ranks of house officers have often been tapped to fill openings for assistant managers on the floor, and some house officers have advanced to the position of hotel manager.

Banquet and Catering Department

Since the banquet department is primarily concerned with food and its service, one might think that it belongs in the back of the house. But since hotel banquet departments deal directly with guests or groups desiring space for conventions, meetings, luncheons, dinners, and other functions, the banquet department is considered front of the house.

In many hotels, banquet and catering functions make up a large portion of the profit from food operation. Group banquet business results in considerable revenue, not only from food and liquor sales, but from room rentals as well. Hotels with inadequate banquet facilities stand to lose a considerable amount of room business.

Associations and business groups require a large amount of public space for exhibits and meetings at their annual conventions. They also need adequate ballroom and public space to accommodate the general luncheons, dinners, and meetings held for their membership. Accordingly, when officers of these groups plan their annual conventions, they are guided in their choice of a city and hotel by the size of the facilities available to accommodate their group. For this reason, cities that can provide adequate convention space— including large assembly halls for general meetings and enough small meeting rooms for divisional meetings—attract this large group business. Cities like New York, Atlantic City, Chicago, San Francisco, St. Louis, Miami, Dallas, Fort Worth, Boston, Washington, DC, New Orleans, and others even have special bureaus to solicit such group business. Because it results in extra billions of dollars in revenue for their hotels, restaurants, amusements, theaters, stores, and transportation facilities, cities vie for this convention business.

Such large group business results in concentrated service and good profits, and hotels seek to obtain as much of this business as possible. Banquet facilities and the operation of the banquet department figure largely in how much large group business an individual hotel receives.

Banquet Manager

The banquet manager supervises this department and is usually responsible to both the catering manager and the director of sales. The reason is because the banquet manager fulfills two functions: one as a food manager and the other as a salesperson. Many hotels have made the banquet department part of the sales department, although it operates independently.

All arrangements for banquets and other social functions are overseen by the banquet manager, who directs the physical setups of the functions, draws up and signs contracts, and suggests or arranges for entertainment. In addition, the banquet manager works in coordination with all other departments involved in serving group business, such as the front office (rooms), sales department (which may have brought this business to the hotel), housekeeping, and others. The banquet manager is responsible for the efficient operation of all functions at the affair and must see to it that the hotel carries out its part of the bargain.

Banquet work is highly specialized and requires experience not only in planning menus and arranging meeting and convention setups, but also in food costing and control. A banquet manager must know how to eliminate costly items from banquet menus without reducing the quality or appearance of the meal. He or she must know how to increase the sale of profit-bearing food and liquor and be able to sell his or her personality and ability to guests and committees.

The banquet manager can reach this position by starting at the bottom and learning each phase of food operation on the way up, or he or she can prepare to work in this department by taking special educational and culinary courses. In some hotels, promotion to banquet manager is made from the sales department, chef-steward's office, or managerial staff.

Banquet Staff

The size of the banquet staff is determined by the size of the hotel and its banquet operations. Their duties include selling space, scheduling events, keeping date books to avoid duplications of bookings, arranging for the listing of daily and weekly events on bulletin boards, suggesting and making up sample menus, arranging all functions for social events, setting up menus and programs, and servicing all functions.

Successful banquet personnel are trained in food and hotel operations. Many excellent schools specialize in food and restaurant control and operation, at both the associate and bachelor's degree levels. Most graduates start out in the chef-steward's department or as a beginner in the banquet department. The chef-steward's department is preferable because it offers better groundwork in food preparation, cost, administration, and menu preparation. Many who have succeeded in the banquet field began as assistant waiters or waiters in hotel or outside restaurants. Food experience is important not only to success in the banquet department, but also to future success in any hotel career.

Banquet departments also include the wait staff, which is supervised by the banquet headwaiter. Banquet waiters and waitresses are specially trained in banquet operations, which differ from regular table waiting. To aid the wait staff, there are assistant waiters and waitresses and housekeepers who set up tables, bars, and buffets before service begins. The housekeepers clear out furnishings after each function.

Educational requirements for these positions are not rigid. If you cannot pursue advanced training, you can learn the basics of food operation by working in food departments. If you start as an assistant waiter or waitress, however, do not rely exclusively on this kind of on-the-job training. Once you have gotten your foot in the door, make arrangements to augment your practical experience with courses in food costs, control, preparation, and operation. Also add courses in hotel management and operation. These will help round out your experience and facilitate your advancement. Many successful hotel executives started out on the lower rungs of banquet operations. Opportunity is yours here, and your advancement will depend upon your own education, personality, ability, energy, ambition, and will to succeed.

It is helpful for a waiter to have a good memory to avoid confusing customers' orders and to recall faces, names, and preferences of frequent patrons. These workers also should be comfortable using computers to place orders and generate customers' bills. Some may need to be quick at arithmetic so they can total bills manually. Knowledge of a foreign language is helpful to communicate with the diverse clientele and staff of many hotels.

Hours and Earnings

The workweek in the banquet and catering departments has no set hours, as do other departments; the schedule is staggered. Since most functions take place in the evening, banquet employees are frequently asked to come in late and stay late. The hours will vary greatly even from day to day.

Although salaries in hotel banquet and catering departments are generally higher than in other dining establishments, it is difficult to estimate the average earnings for wait staff and other such personnel, since their incomes depend upon the amount of business booked and the amount of tips they receive. Banquet work also can be seasonal (summer weddings and winter holiday parties, for example), and earnings can fluctuate widely.

In 2002, median hourly earnings (including tips) of waiters and waitresses overall were $6.80. The middle 50 percent earned between $6.13 and $8.00; the lowest 10 percent earned less than $5.70; and the highest 10 percent earned more than $11.00 an hour. For most waiters and waitresses, higher earnings are primarily the result of receiving more in tips rather than higher hourly wages. Tips usually average between 10 and 20 percent of guests' checks; waiters and waitresses working in busy, expensive restaurants earn the most. Banquet managers had average earnings of $40,182.

In some large restaurants and hotels, food and beverage servers as well as related workers belong to unions, principally the Hotel Employees and Restaurant Employees International Union and the Service Employees International Union.

5

The Front of the House: Business Departments and Management

In this chapter we will consider accounting, credit, purchasing, central files, human resources, public relations and advertising, sales and marketing, and management. These are the departments that comprise the remainder of front-of-the-house operations.

Accounting Department

Although its members are not generally in direct contact with guests, the accounting department is included in front-of-the-house operations because much of the work is managerial and accounting executives often advance to top hotel positions. A separate department, which reports directly to the manager, frequently handles all accounting functions.

As in other businesses, the accounting department supervises the financial affairs of the organization. Accounting duties include fiscal policy and planning, maintenance of fiscal records and accounts, preparation of regular periodical and annual financial statements, control of expenditures, and the recording of income, maintenance of bank accounts, and handling of payrolls.

In small hotels the owner-manager may keep a set of simple books that are regularly checked or supervised by outside accountants. In larger hotels, however, accounting operations are huge and complicated and require large staffs to maintain them.

Specialized education and training are needed for work in the accounting department. At least a high school education is required for entry-level positions, and if you plan to further your career in this specialized field, it will be necessary to obtain a bachelor's degree in accounting and perhaps even become a certified public accountant. Top spots here, as auditor or controller, require strong accounting backgrounds.

If you plan a career in hotel accounting, specialize in accounting at school before entering hotel work. Then, at least, you will have the foundation for a position as controller or auditor. Working your way up is the next step.

Controller

This is a highly specialized position, and most accountants reach it only after extensive experience, preferably in the hotel business. The controller—or chief accountant, as this position is called in some hotels—not only heads the operation of the accounting department, but is also closely affiliated with operations and executive management. Many hotel owners and operators consider hotel accounting a highly specialized field and accordingly will entrust the affairs of their hotels only to accountants with considerable hotel experience. They believe that service operations and time-and-cost accounting are so different from other businesses that only a hotel accountant can successfully do the job.

Auditor

Internal auditors verify the accuracy of the hotel's internal records and check for mismanagement, waste, or fraud. In this increasingly important area of accounting, auditors examine and evaluate the firm's financial and information systems, management procedures, and internal controls to ensure that records are accurate and controls are adequate to protect against fraud and waste.

As computer systems make information timelier, internal auditors help managers to base their decisions on actual data, rather than personal observation. Internal auditors also may recommend controls for their organization's computer system to ensure the reliability of the system and the integrity of the data.

Auditors also review company operations, evaluating their efficiency, effectiveness, and compliance with corporate policies and procedures, laws, and government regulations. Auditors working for hotels must have a degree in accounting and experience in the particular aspects of the hotel industry and the laws and regulations that govern it. As with the controller, promotion to auditor comes after many years of hotel experience. From auditor, the next step up is promotion to controller.

Auditing clerk is an entry-level position. Auditing clerks verify records of transactions posted by other workers. They check figures, postings, and documents to ensure that they are correct, mathematically accurate, and properly coded. They also correct or note errors for accountants or other workers to adjust.

Accounts Payable

The accounts payable division is responsible for checking bills presented against shipping invoices and receipts, and then authorizing payment. In some hotels, accounts payable may draw checks and even have authority to sign and issue them.

A high school education is the minimum requirement for positions in accounts payable. Accounting, bookkeeping, and other business training are also required in many hotels. Some openings as clerks do exist for beginners, and high school graduates generally fill these.

Promotion from accounts payable to the auditing staff is possible if you possess the proper education and business training. A college degree is highly desirable. Promotion is also possible to the credit, front office, and purchasing departments. From here, too, you can go up the ladder to a position in management.

Accounts Receivable

The accounts receivable section lists payments and keeps records of all money received. This division records all room, restaurant, and other charges made by guests, as well as payments of these and other charges.

The systems employed by accounts receivable departments differ among hotels. In some establishments, cashiers keep ledgers and do their own postings. In others, all charge slips are forwarded to the accounts receivable department where entries are made. The procedures vary depending on the size of the hotel and the system set up by the controller and auditor.

Opportunities for positions here correspond closely with those in accounts payable, and educational and training requirements are also the same. Consequently, promotions possible in the accounts payable department are also possible in the accounts receivable department.

Payroll

Payment of all wages and salaries, maintenance of payroll records, the issuance of payroll checks, and the coordination of the payroll disbursements against wage and hour scales are the responsibility of the payroll department.

The paymaster is in charge of his or her department, and promotion to this position is generally from the accounting and credit departments, although some hotels may employ paymasters with experience in other hotels or businesses.

Assisting the paymaster are the following positions:

- Payroll clerks create and issue paychecks, compute wage and hour scales, keep records, check timekeeper reports, and perform other functions of the paymaster.
- Payroll cashiers issue checks to employees.
- Payroll conciliation clerks check the payroll bank account regularly to make certain that there is sufficient cash on deposit to meet all payroll accounts.
- Various miscellaneous positions in the payroll department will assist with other duties and responsibilities as necessary.

Education and training requirements are general and somewhat similar to those of accounts payable and receivable. Studies in accounting, bookkeeping, statistics, hour and wage computation, personnel, and other affiliated courses are recommended.

Since many functions of the payroll department are clerical, there are opportunities here for beginners. There are also many opportunities for advancement and for gaining experience.

Other Opportunities in Accounting

There are opportunities for employment in the accounting department other than those just described. Depending upon the size of the hotel, there are certain other duties and functions that the controller or accounting department is responsible for. The scope of the accounting department's job responsibilities varies from one hotel to the next.

Large hotels usually maintain statistical departments that correlate pertinent data helpful for the future operation of the hotel. The statistical department records such data as these:

- Registrations, which are used to ascertain where guests come from, the percentages of the geographical derivation of business, and other geographical data
- Food and liquor purchases by brand, dish, age of customer, or other breakdowns deemed important by management
- Age group and gender of guests
- Returns from advertising and promotion campaigns
- Time study and payroll information

This information is put to use by the purchasing department, the chef, the front office, advertising, sales and sales promotion, public relations, and other executive offices.

In many hotels, the accounting department has supervision of room and restaurant cashiers, and the house treasurer or chief cashier is responsible for all duties assigned to cashiers. Cashiers perform all the duties their title implies. They receive payments, post charges, make change, and keep daily records.

In some hotels, the accounting department controls food purchasing; in other hotels it is part of the chef-steward's department or purchasing department. In large hotels, both of these departments, as well as the accounting department, may employ control and verification personnel who double-check and correlate each other's figures. Ultimately, the accounting department will check all purchasing and chef-steward accounts for errors and will make certain all records have been properly entered.

Hours and Earnings

Personnel in the accounting department generally work eight hours a day, five or six days a week. Conditions of employment here are similar to regular office work.

Accounting work provides an excellent background in hotel management and operation. The supervision of financial matters is an important function, and the controller of the hotel probably is more informed about its costs, problems, and other operations than any other person in the hotel. Every financial transaction passes before this person. Many a controller has become manager of a hotel. It is a logical promotion.

Educational requirements are high for employment and advancement in the accounting department. A minimum of a high school education is required for entry-level positions. A college degree is needed for higher than clerical positions. While there are openings as clerks available to beginners, most employees are required to have some form of bookkeeping or accounting background.

Median hourly earnings of full-time accounting, bookkeeping, and auditing clerks were $13.16 in 2002, depending on the job and its responsibilities. Payroll clerks averaged $13.96 per hour. Jobs further up the ladder vary greatly in remuneration, as there are many factors to be taken into consideration that are not common to all hotels. The rate of income will depend on the size of the department, hotel, and city; the responsibilities; the volume of business; and the kind of system set up by the controller. In general, earnings here are as good as, if not higher than, those in most hotel departments. Sometimes meals are provided for managers or other members of the department.

According to the *Hospitality Compensation Exchange 2002 Lodging Property Annual Report* (http://hospitalitycareernet.com/career resources/lodgporp.asp), controllers can expect to earn anywhere from $67,000 to $159,000 per year, depending on the size of the facility.

Credit Department

The credit department is responsible for authorizing charges made by guests, making adjustments on statements when incorrect charges have been posted, and keeping records and files of all credit transactions. Credit departments determine the credit limit of guests in most hotels and indicate this on credit cards by key letters or numerals.

A credit manager, who supervises assistants in performing the main functions, is in charge of this department. Promotion to credit manager is usually from assistantships in the credit department. The position carries a great deal of responsibility, and candidates are very carefully considered. It is rare for an outsider without hotel experience to be brought into this job. Hotels are frequently judged in industry circles by the reliability of their credit methods and judgments.

In some larger hotels, credit investigators work with the assistant credit manager. It is their duty to check accounts where credit has been overextended, investigate fraud, and, in general, oversee credit operations to prevent any criminal action against the hotel.

The credit department supervises operation of a "guest history" section for the sales department in some hotels. This section records the special requests and particular likes of guests, information that is cross-filed so that these special desires can be noted instantly against reservation or registration cards. A guest history might include requests such as that for an extralong bed, four pillows, a room with southern exposure, or a room no higher than five floors above street level. The history also includes other pertinent information, such as the number of stays per year of each guest, the time of year the guest usually checks in, and so on. This information helps the sales department decide whom to favor in peak periods. To aid the credit department in its work, the guest history section may also include names of delinquent accounts and bad credit risks. In these cases, arrivals or reservations are noted instantly by the credit department and preventive action can be taken.

Work hours in the credit department are based on the three-shift system. In large hotels, there is always someone on night duty. In smaller hotels, the general cashier or the owner-manager will assume these functions.

A high school education, and preferably a college degree, is required in this department. Since there is much responsibility placed on the members of the credit office, most hotels are generally unwilling to employ people for credit work who have had no experience or education. When openings occur here, other employees of the hotel are considered, with education and background being important factors. From credit, promotions are made to front office or managerial staff.

Starting salaries in the credit department are about the same as in general accounting, depending on the size of the hotel and other factors. Regular increases augment the earnings here, and in some hotels, meals are provided managers and assistant managers.

Purchasing Department

The purchasing department, while actually a back-of-the-house operation, is included in this front-of-the-house section since it performs a largely managerial function. The acumen of the purchasing manager and the efficiency of the purchasing department can make for the profitable operation of a hotel.

Duties of the purchasing department include interviewing salespeople, placing orders for goods needed by all hotel departments, keeping records of all purchases and payments, drawing up and signing contracts and agreements for the purchase of all goods, comparing price and quality on all bids received, receiving and checking the quality and quantity of merchandise received on all orders, checking receipts and shipping invoices against accounts payable and then forwarding any such information to the accounting department, suggesting changes in the use of certain goods where costs can be saved or quality improved, and suggesting new products.

In some hotels, heads of both the housekeeping and the chef-steward departments conduct their own interviews with sales representatives, place and check orders, and perform other functions generally handled by the purchasing staff. This generally depends on the hotel's size and its management structure.

The head of this department is the director of purchasing, sometimes called purchasing agent. This director oversees the functions of the purchasing staff, and responsibilities include interviewing, training, disciplining, and discharging employees. Promotion to purchasing director is usually from staff positions within the department. Occasionally a hotel may hire a purchasing agent who has had considerable purchasing experience in other hotels or other businesses.

Experience in purchasing, merchandising, and associated fields provides an excellent background for purchasing work in hotels. Specialization in some particular phase of purchasing is sometimes also required as, for example, the purchasing of canned goods, office supplies, food, liquor, or linens. In some hotels, employees from other departments are considered for advancement to jobs in the purchasing department. Promotion will depend largely upon the individual, his or her education and experience, and the responsibility of the opening.

Purchasing checkers handle invoice control, examine incoming invoices to check errors, check invoices against purchasing department records and purchase orders, and verify the quality and quantity of all goods received. They also notify the purchasing agent of vendors' compliance with all of the terms of purchasing orders and contracts.

A high school education is generally required for employment in this department, and college or hotel training courses are preferred. While such beginners' jobs as clerks, secretaries, and office helpers occur in the purchasing department, opportunities for better jobs and promotions depend upon experience, ability, and training. Other fields in which experience can be gained are selling and estimating.

Most purchasing department employees work eight hours a day for five or six days a week. In general, office help will be on duty

9:00 a.m. to 5:00 p.m., while checkers or other helpers who are concerned with incoming shipments may work staggered or late hours to meet these shipments.

According to the *Hospitality Compensation Exchange 2002 Lodging Property Annual Report* (http://hospitalitycareernet.com/career resources/lodgprop.asp), directors of purchasing had average annual earnings of $48,787. Earnings for purchasing clerks are similar to those of clerks in the various payroll divisions.

Central Files Department

A central files department is usually found only in large hotels, where files are most often kept on computer databases. In small hotels, other departments absorb these functions, as the number of files doesn't warrant establishing a special division.

As the files kept by large hotels have increased, it has become inefficient for each department to keep its own files. As a result, the central file system was set up. It includes a central sorting and clearing center where all files are sorted, duplications are weeded out, and central mailing lists are set up. Computers have further streamlined much of the work of the central files staff. Files kept might include general correspondence, bulletins, executive memorandums, contracts, guest files, and other information.

In some hotels, the duties of the general storekeeper and interoffice mailroom have been incorporated into the central files division. The general storekeeper stocks and issues all office supplies, maintaining inventory as needed. The interoffice mailroom distributes all interoffice correspondence and handles the mailing of all hotel mail and packages. This central mailing center not only saves the time of different departments, but also helps keep one central control over all postal expenditures. In large hotels, postage is an expensive item.

The chief file clerk supervises the work of this department, and positions here include file clerks, mail personnel, storekeeper, and assistants. No special educational requirements are needed, although at least a high school education is preferred and an understanding of computers is helpful. Many hotels give part-time employment here to students attending hotel training schools.

Promotion from the central files is possible to other departments of the hotel. The chief file clerk's position is a skilled position, since knowledge of filing systems and controls is necessary. The chief file clerk is appointed from other file clerks or from another department of the hotel. Occasionally, a hotel will employ as chief file clerk someone who has had filing experience in other hotels or businesses.

Earnings in this department depend on the size of the hotel. In general, file clerks earn approximately the same as clerks in the accounting department.

Human Resources Department

In large hotels, separate departments handle various aspects of human resources management duties. These duties include keeping files on all employees; interviewing applicants for positions; advising applicants of their fitness for the various openings in the hotel; keeping time records; investigating the references of all applicants; recording changes in employees' earnings, hours, jobs, education, training, home addresses, or telephone numbers; recording employee absences; and noting merits, bonuses, disciplinary comments, recommendations from department heads, and causes for discharge. Human resources work also includes supplying references to other companies requesting information about previous employees, keeping lists of employees being considered for promotion, and supervising assignment and control of lockers. In addition, the human resources staff analyzes the various jobs in the hotel to determine what special requirements or characteristics are most needed to perform them well.

One key position in the department is that of timekeeper, who reports to the paymaster. It is the timekeeper's responsibility to record the time of employees' arrivals and departures where there are no time clocks. He or she fills out time sheets, services the time clock, and performs other related duties. The timekeeper's reports are used by human resources, for records, and by the paymaster, for computing payroll.

Because a considerable number of hotel employees wear uniforms, most hotels provide lockers and dressing rooms where employees can change clothes. The human resources department locker crew regularly checks employee lockers, replacing locks when employees resign or are discharged and repairing lockers as needed. The crew also keeps track of articles of value left behind in the dressing room or in unlocked lockers.

The head of this department—typically called the director of human resources—supervises all these personnel functions. While many directors have worked their way up, most hotels demand people with special education and training in human resources work. In most cases, a college education is required of applicants for this department, and is a necessity for the position of director. Many colleges today have special courses of study in personnel and human resources. Promotion from personnel director is straight up the ladder and may lead toward a managerial office.

Working under the director are managers and specialists in various aspects of human resources management. The main divisions of a typical human resources department are employment, recruitment, equal employment opportunity (EEO), compensation and benefits, employee relations, and labor relations. Each of these areas requires general knowledge of employee relations practices, and some fields, such as EEO and labor relations, require specialized training.

Opportunities to enter the human resources department may be offered to persons who have not had hotel experience, but who have the proper educational and work experience. In some instances, hotels will promote other workers to positions in this department. Conversely, employees in the human resources department are eligible for promotion to other departments where openings exist. By the nature of their work in personnel analysis and job evaluation, human resources workers learn a great deal about hotel operation. The experience to be gained in this department is invaluable in starting a hotel career.

Earnings in human resources vary depending on the employee's area of expertise, experience, and education. According to the *Hospitality Compensation Exchange 2002 Lodging Property Annual Report* (http://hospitalitycareernet.com/careerresources/lodgprop.asp), directors of human resources received average annual earnings of $58,677; assistant directors averaged $43,330.

Public Relations and Advertising Department

Public relations (PR) and advertising are specialties in their own rights. Most hotels fill openings in these departments with personnel who have gained PR experience in other hotels or industries. While advertising procedures and practices are fairly similar in hotels and in other businesses, public relations procedures for hotels are somewhat specialized.

The tasks and problems that confront employees in hotel public relations are quite varied. For example, on one day the PR executive might prepare a program for a technical education group; the next day he or she might publicize a variety show in the hotel's main dining room. In large hotels, the director plans and supervises sales promotion activities in addition to supervising any public relations programs.

Hotel public relations representatives are really executive assistants to top management. They are constantly called upon to represent and speak for the executive branch of the hotel. They must have a complete understanding of general hotel operation and policies, and must know what is required of each worker in the hotel and the hour and wage schedule of every department. A public relations executive—the title may be either manager or director—must have a bachelor's degree, experience, and good judgment.

Public relations is an important profession in the hotel industry when you realize that a hotel primarily sells service, something so intangible that it must be measured solely in terms of public acceptance and recognition.

Advertising operations in a hotel are similar to those of any other business. The advertising manager or an outside agency prepares newspaper and magazine copy and suggests the appropriate media. The advertising manager in a hotel is also responsible for internal displays, such as those in elevators, on lobby easels, on window displays, on dining room table cards, and others. This person also supervises the printing of menus, programs for banquet functions, and all other printing, including stationery, business cards, billheads, ledger cards, and so forth.

Most advertising and public relations jobs go to people who have had some experience in these fields. College education is usually required. However, there are opportunities to enter these professions as an apprentice and to gain on-the-job experience. This will depend purely upon the size of the hotel and of the advertising and public relations staffs.

Remuneration varies with the hotel. In 2002, public relations specialists overall had average hourly earnings of $23.11; advertising agents averaged $20.93. According to the *Hospitality Compensation Exchange 2002 Lodging Property Annual Report* (http://hospitalitycareernet.com/careerresources/lodgprop.asp), directors of public relations had average annual earnings of $71,523.

Sales and Marketing Department

Selling space in public rooms and bringing large group business to the hotel is the responsibility of the sales department. The volume of sales, and work, depends on the amount of space and other public facilities available.

Sales management has become an integral part of hotel operation and management. With sales in this industry now assuming a major position of importance, the sales director is regularly consulted regarding hotel policy and operation. In the larger chains, he or she is responsible only to the managing director or president and has complete authority and responsibility for front office, restaurant, banquet, and management policy.

This authority is easily understood when you consider that sales is the department actively going after business. The sales department is in charge of all advertising and promotional expenditures; it determines which market should be exploited to realize the best results in room and food sales for the hotel.

Hotel sales personnel are essentially the same as sales forces in any business. While there are no specified educational requirements, a high school education, at least, is preferred, and a college education is necessary for future advancement. Completion of special courses in hotel management and operation will benefit persons interested in furthering their careers in sales work.

Sales departments differ with the various hotels. Some hotels may appoint one person as the director of sales or sales manager and label the rest of the staff as assistant sales managers, while other hotels have given these assistant sales directors such individual titles as sales manager, convention manager, merchandise manager, and foreign sales manager. In the latter case, each salesperson specializes only in the type of business her or his title implies. While the convention manager goes after conventions, the merchandise manager goes after buyers and mercantile firms. However, the current trend in hotel sales work is away from this subdivision of departmental activities. Often certain business prospects lead to others, and it is not efficient to shift people according to the type of business.

Sales representatives, like credit staff, are often given assistant manager titles since this aids them in their contacts. Many businesses have found it advantageous to appoint numerous vice presidents in their sales departments for the same reason.

The sales director or manager has the duty of assigning leads or accounts to the various salespeople. Many salespeople receive percentage bonuses in addition to their salaries, and the sales manager must avoid favoritism in assigning accounts. The sales director must also work to maintain a good relationship with other departments in the hotel.

For example, close liaison between sales and banquet departments is required. Since the major portion of sales involves those of public space, the work of both departments must be closely coordinated. To prevent duplicate bookings, one master entry book is usually kept. Once an event has been booked, the salesperson alone, or with the parties concerned present, arranges the setup, menu, and other details of the affair or function with the banquet manager.

The sales force also works very closely with the public relations department since sales promotion is one of this department's functions in many hotels. And even in those hotels where sales promotions (as in industry) are handled by a separate department, public relations work is generally called for with each group, including program advice and planning, press releases, speech writing, publicity, special events, photography arrangements, and other customary duties of public relations.

Beginners may enter the sales department directly from the outside, although front office clerks, credit staff, accounting personnel, banquet representatives, bellhops, and others are often considered when openings occur in sales departments. Important characteristics sought by hotels in their salespeople are intelligence, good appearance, and the ability not only to sell to people, but to get along with them as well.

Working hours are staggered. Many contacts are made at social affairs or dinner parties, and sales reps frequently have to work evenings to develop business. Then, too, many prospects have their own business to occupy them in the daytime and are available for sales presentations only in the evenings. Along with irregular hours, hotel salespeople spend time on the road, contacting association officers and businesspeople at meetings and conventions in other cities.

One is usually promoted to managerial work from sales work. As the one who brings in the business, the salesperson has a following and, therefore, has a particular value, especially after many years of experience.

In 2002, nonsupervisory employees in advertising and public relations averaged $602 per week. Median salaries for marketing managers were $78,250; for sales managers the average was $75,040. Some managers also receive bonuses in addition to their regular salaries.

Frank W. Berkman, former director of the Hotel Sales Management Association International (HSMAI), outlined the role of the sales and marketing departments in a hotel's success. Mr. Berkman, a certified hospitality marketing executive (CHME) who worked in sales and hotel management for many years, writes:

> The hospitality industry today, more than ever before, offers unlimited opportunities for anyone seeking a challenging, stimulating, and rewarding career. In many countries throughout the world, as well as in numerous areas and provinces in the United States and Canada, the combined hospitality-tourism field is either the first- or second-largest industry in terms of business volume.
>
> Hotels, motels, and resorts have a dramatic impact on all sections of economic, social, and cultural life. . . . To encourage and further expand this use, whether it is business or pleasure-oriented, and to continually secure profitable levels of room, food, and beverage sales—are all primary functions of sales and marketing.
>
> There is a certain glamour and allure associated with hotel/ motel sales promotion, advertising, publicity, and public relations. These include opportunities to meet famous and fascinating people from all walks of life, to travel, to entertain, as well as status and prestige, excellent industry advancement, and high salary potentials. Perhaps more significant are the unique opportunities hotel/motel sales and marketing can offer you in the fulfillment of your own very personal career wants and needs.
>
> For example, ask yourself these questions: Would I enjoy the challenge of motivating people to purchase useful services or products, particularly by face-to-face selling? Would I particularly like the areas of business management and administration . . . of being in charge of an active, productive sales office? Do I especially seek out opportunities to use my creative abilities? Am I better suited to detail work—such as that involved with proper servicing after the sale is made?

If your answer to any of these questions is yes, then there certainly is a profitable place and a satisfying career for you in hotel/motel sales and marketing.

Job Titles

If you are interested in hotel/motel sales and marketing, then what kind of place and what specific job might you look for? The following offers a brief description of just some of the wide variety of challenging career positions in hotel sales and marketing.

- **Vice president of marketing**—Establishes annual marketing program aimed at developing maximum business volume for rooms, food, beverages, and other sales; prepares sales goals and budgets; trains and develops sales personnel; supervises and coordinates all related activities such as direct selling, advertising, publicity, and public relations
- **Director of sales**—Administers, coordinates, and supervises sales department executives who are responsible for soliciting and servicing conventions, sales meetings, tours, and other groups requiring public space and room accommodations; creates and implements programs aimed at stimulating individual room, food, and beverage business
- **Director of advertising**—Develops coordinated advertising campaigns and programs involving newspapers, magazines, radio and television, outdoor advertising, and direct mail; works closely with advertising agencies in the creation and production of advertising and promotional literature
- **Director of public relations**—Responsible for developing positive programs directed at maximizing the hotel's image and its relations with the community, its employees, its guests, and the general public

- **International sales manager**—Coordinates activities specifically aimed at stimulating and developing both individual and group business from areas outside the country
- **Tour and agency manager**—Responsible for developing both group and individual business through personal contacts with travel agents, tour operators, transportation companies, and carrier representatives
- **Convention service manager**—Coordinates all hotel departments to ensure maximum service to conventions and other groups once they are in the hotel and is responsible for supervising all in-house activities of the groups that involve hotel services
- **Sales representative**—Directly contacts both repeat and new business prospects on a regularly established basis— through personal visits, telephone calls, and direct mail—for the specific purpose of booking a continuing flow of profitable business

The need for qualified sales personnel is an ever-present one. New hotel/motel/resort construction, the resulting increase in competition, and the ever-expanding market potentials—both domestic and international—all help make the experienced, professional sales and marketing executive one of the most sought-after employees in the hospitality industry.

A wide range of educational backgrounds is suitable for advertising, marketing, promotions, public relations, and sales managerial jobs, but many employers prefer those with experience in related occupations plus a broad liberal arts background. A bachelor's degree in liberal arts is generally acceptable. As with other occupations in the hotel industry, specialized training in hotel management will give you an advantage.

But because of the unique nature of the hospitality industry, there are a number of special qualities that are essential for those desiring to be successful in the selling and servicing of its products. They are:

- **Empathy**—The ability to put yourself in the other person's place, such as when motivating a customer to buy by appealing to his or her specific needs and wants
- **Initiative**—The capacity of being a self-starter, to seek out and explore new business sources and potentials
- **Creativity**—The capacity to develop new, special, or unique marketing programs, attractions, or selling techniques, so that the benefits of your particular property stand out among all others

Although nothing can take the place of actual on-the-job experience, there are ample opportunities for those of you in high school and college, for example, to help build a proper foundation for your hotel career. Be sure to include in your curriculum courses in sales promotion, advertising, marketing, merchandising, tourism, motivation, communications, and public speaking. Actively participate in sales seminars and marketing workshops, such as those conducted by the Hotel Sales and Marketing Association International for both industry and colleges. And, HSMAI student membership is highly recommended as an extremely low-cost means of obtaining information on all facets of sales and marketing. The organization also offers educational opportunities to all levels of sales and marketing professionals. Visit the HSMAI website at www.hsmai .org for information.

Operating Management

The resident manager is operating head of the hotel who supervises and directs all activities of the various departments. Generally he or she is also on the executive board and is responsible only to the president or managing director of the hotel. The overall responsibility of the resident manager is to see that the guests are satisfied and that the hotel is operated as cleanly and as profitably as possible.

The resident manager has authority to appoint or discharge any employee or department head for inefficiency, misconduct, or any other valid reason. He or she carries out the policies originated by the executive board or managing director and plans their execution by the various departments. At regularly held meetings of the department heads, the resident manager introduces policy, schedules, and the execution of plans and discusses interdepartmental problems and conflicts. The resident manager also issues regular bulletins or notices to department heads and all other employees, notifying them of new policies, changes in operating schedules, hotel activities, and functions of interest.

As operating head of the hotel, the resident manager also participates in final negotiations with labor unions or employee groups after initial discussions and agreements have been prepared by the personnel department of the hotel.

The resident manager and the executive management must also be well experienced in the engineering functions of the hotel. Building and operating equipment problems, while under the direct surveillance of the chief engineer, are important management problems as well. Managers must be familiar with the most efficient types of machinery; they should understand furnaces, laundry machinery, kitchen machinery, and other equipment necessary to hotel operation. Although they need not be expert on such matters, resident managers should nevertheless understand these problems well enough to prevent inefficiency in engineering practices. Many schools give special courses in hotel engineering to better acquaint management students with this important and expensive back-of-the-house problem.

Assistant and executive assistant managers work under the general manager; their number is determined by the size of the hotel. In general hotel practice, executive assistants are on duty during each of the three shifts. Representing the manager, they are empowered to act officially in all situations coming to their attention.

In smaller hotels, the owner—usually the manager—may assume not only all the responsibilities of resident manager, but also those of the front office, credit, human resources, and other departments. Since the problems of small hotel operation are not considered the same as those of larger hotels, experience for resident manager openings in large hotels is best obtained in large hotel operations.

Training, Advancement, and Earnings

Hotels increasingly emphasize specialized training, especially for managerial positions. Postsecondary training in hotel or restaurant management is preferred for most hotel management positions, although a college liberal arts degree may be sufficient when coupled with related hotel experience. Internships or part-time or even summer work are an asset to students seeking a career in hotel management. The experience gained and the contacts made with these employers can greatly benefit students after graduation. Most bachelor's degree programs include work-study opportunities.

Resident managers must be able to get along with many different people, even in stressful situations. They must be able to solve problems and concentrate on details. Initiative, self-discipline, effective communication skills, and the ability to organize and direct the work of others also are essential for managers at all levels.

In the past, many managers were promoted from the ranks of front desk clerks, housekeepers, waiters, chefs, and hotel sales workers. Although some employees still advance to hotel management positions without education beyond high school, postsecondary education is preferred. Restaurant management training or experience also is a good background for entering hotel management, because the success of a hotel's food service and beverage operations often is important to the profitability of the entire establishment.

Graduates of hotel or restaurant management programs usually start their careers as trainee assistant managers. Some large hotels sponsor specialized on-the-job management training programs that allow trainees to rotate among various departments and gain a thorough knowledge of the hotel's operation. Other hotels may help finance formal training in hotel management for outstanding employees. Newly built hotels, particularly those without established on-the-job training programs, often prefer to hire applicants who have hotel management experience.

Large hotel and motel chains may offer better opportunities for advancement than small, independently owned establishments, but relocation every several years often is necessary for advancement. The large chains have more extensive career-ladder programs and offer managers the opportunity to transfer to another hotel or motel in the chain or to the central office. Career advancement can be accelerated by the completion of certification programs offered by various associations. These programs usually require a combination of course work, examinations, and experience. For example, outstanding lodging managers may advance to higher-level manager positions.

Salaries of lodging managers vary greatly according to their responsibilities and the segment of the hotel industry in which they are employed, as well as the location and region where the hotel is located. According to the Hospitality Compensation Exchange 2002 Lodging Property Annual Report, resident managers had average annual earnings of $74,181. Managers may earn bonuses of up to 25 percent of their basic salary in some hotels and also may be furnished with lodging, meals, parking, laundry, and other services. In addition to providing typical benefits, some hotels offer profit-sharing plans and educational assistance to their employees.

Top Management

In the largest hotels, where operations rest in the hands of a resident manager and her or his staff, executive policy and control is in the hands of a higher executive branch. This may consist of a chief executive officer, chief operating officer, and board of directors. These executives represent ownership of the hotel or chain.

The executive, or group, formulates policy and supervises the actions of the resident manager. Although mostly concerned with financial matters and the accounting of profits or losses, the executive branch will take part in operational functions when called upon by the resident manager, or when conditions arise to make intervention necessary.

The executive management also arranges for financing when needed, decides on important changes in operations, approves investments for improvement or other reasons, hires top personnel, and, in general, supervises all top-level operations. Resident managers may be appointed to an executive post. Quite commonly, members of the executive board are chosen from banks, insurance companies, or other business groups that have financial or other interests in the hotel.

Training, Advancement, and Earnings

The formal education and experience of top executives varies as widely as the nature of their responsibilities. Many top executives have a bachelor's or higher degree in business administration or liberal arts. Because many top executive positions are filled by promoting experienced, lower-level managers when an opening occurs, many top managers have been promoted from within the hotel organization. As we have seen throughout this book, it is sometimes possible for individuals without a college degree to work their way up within the hotel and become managers. However, many hotels prefer that their top executives have specialized backgrounds and, therefore, hire individuals who have specific experience.

Top executives must have highly developed personal skills. An analytical mind able to quickly assess large amounts of information and data is very important, as is the ability to consider and evaluate the interrelationships of numerous factors. Top executives also must be able to communicate clearly and persuasively. Other qualities critical for managerial success include leadership, self-confidence, motivation, decisiveness, flexibility, sound business judgment, and determination.

Managers can help advance their careers by becoming familiar with the latest developments in management techniques at national or local training programs sponsored by various industry and trade associations. Participation in conferences and seminars can expand knowledge of national and international issues influencing the organization and can help the participants to develop a network of useful contacts.

General managers may advance to top executive positions, such as executive vice president. They may even advance to peak corporate positions such as chief operating officer or chief executive officer. Chief executive officers often become members of the board of directors of one or more firms, typically as a director of their own firm and often as chair of its board of directors. Some top executives establish their own firms or become independent consultants.

Earnings for top executives vary depending on the level of responsibility, length of service, and size and location of the hotel. The median annual earnings of chief executive officers in all industries in 2002 were $145,600; however, it is not uncommon for the top executives of large hotel corporations to far exceed this amount. In addition to salaries, total compensation often includes stock options, dividends, and other performance bonuses. The use of executive dining rooms and company aircraft and cars, expense allowances, and company-paid insurance premiums and physical examinations also are among benefits commonly enjoyed by top executives in private industry. A number of chief executive officers also are provided with company-paid club memberships, a limousine with chauffeur, and other amenities.

6

THE BACK OF THE HOUSE: FOOD SERVICE, HOUSEKEEPING, AND MAINTENANCE

ALTHOUGH MOST TOP management and executive positions are in the front of the house, the best sources for experience and the most opportunities for advancement are in the back of the house. The *back of the house* refers to those operations of the hotel that deal with housekeeping, food, and engineering that are seldom observed by guests. Even though restaurant operations involve direct contact with guests, they are so integral a part of food operations that they are included in this section.

The Food Service Industry

Knowledge of food operation, control, and service is essential for the profitable operation of a hotel. Because of increased costs of labor and materials, the minimum percentage of room occupancy at which hotels can be operated profitably has risen in recent years. Successful food operations can be a major factor in the making of a profitable hotel.

The most useful knowledge about food is not obtained from books but only from actual experience and training. Complete your studies and prepare for hotel work in special hospitality schools, but also learn restaurant and food management and operation by actually working at it in the kitchen and the dining room. This experience will be a great advantage in furthering your hotel career. Many vocational training programs include opportunities for hands-on training.

One of the best ways to enter the hotel industry (and the restaurant field as well) is through the food and beverage areas, according to Bernard Daly and Tony May, whose D-M Restaurant Corporation operates the internationally famous Rainbow Room and Rainbow Grill, both atop the sixty-fifth floor of Rockefeller Center in New York City. Daly and May, whose company operates a full floor of private rooms that compete with New York's leading hotels for banquet business, said:

> We know of no other business that offers as many opportunities to neophytes just starting out on their careers than the food and beverage field. Opportunities, we mean, that are available to almost everyone who chooses this as a lifetime career, regardless of background, education, or environment.
>
> Many of today's top executives in food and beverage started at the very bottom of the ladder, some with more education and training than others, but all imbued with the same common element—a willingness to work hard and a desire to succeed.
>
> There are, in addition, more chances for beginners to get into the field, and perhaps these opportunities are greater than in many other fields because many of the starting positions are seemingly low—as assistant waiters, dishwashers, kitchen assistants, and similar "laboring" areas. But from these have come some of today's

chefs, stewards, sales executives, and, yes, even managers of hotels and restaurants.

The food service industry is still a pioneer's frontier as a business venture and a profession. Over the last few decades all areas of the food service industry have expanded. Commercial restaurants, industrial and institutional food service, airline food service, hotel dining rooms, and other food service businesses have shown significant growth, creating thousands of new job opportunities.

Given the anticipated growth in the hotel industry, it is clear that food service will also expand in the future. The food service industry is still one of opportunity, perhaps more so than any other field. By the same token, the fact must be stressed that knowledge of the business details—of operations and management—is nowhere more required than in this industry.

In reality, a restaurant operator procures raw materials, manufactures the materials into a finished product, and finally places the product for sale on the market. Such a business process requires exacting knowledge because errors or ignorance can prove to be very costly. Perhaps that is why some of the most successful operators in the industry are those who have come up through the ranks. Regardless of formal education, knowledge and experience gained while working your way up the ladder is extremely valuable and desirable.

However, promotion is not easily attained. Competition for advanced positions is keen. As the industry matures, such competition will become even more pronounced. The axiom that advancement must be earned holds true in this industry as much as in any other. Education and training are very important in the food service field. As Bernard Daly and Anthony May stated above, many successful hotel careers began in entry-level food service positions. However, they offer further advice to balance the picture:

This is not to belittle the importance of training and education. Not all chefs, stewards and other food and beverage executives started in lowly positions.

European schools have long been turning out chefs of the highest order. To enter the business with a culinary degree or certificate from a European school, or hotel training course, is tantamount to entering the business world with an M.B.A. from Harvard. . . .

In addition, most of the schools and colleges in this country that turn out finished chefs and kitchen experts have the same aura of attainment as their European counterparts. In many instances, the "connections" made at these American schools of cuisine become important links later on in those hotels and restaurants where previous graduates have important spots.

We heartily recommend the food and beverage area of the industry, because it is first of all extremely challenging and interesting; second, because the preparation and serving of food is self-rewarding; third, because the field is an important one in the hotel and restaurant industry, if not in the entire economy; and last, because success in food and beverage is financially very rewarding at the top.

Food and Liquor Department

The activities of the food and liquor departments are generally supervised by one person. In smaller hotels, the manager or owner may personally supervise these operations. In larger institutions, an executive vice president or a catering director will assume this role. It is this executive's duty to see that all foods purchased meet the requirements of the hotel, the menu, and the food-cost policy. This manager will also supervise the general service in these departments and coordinate operations with other departments as required. This executive must also keep close daily control over these operations so that at all times the operation and food costs are maintained at maximum operating efficiency and to the best advantage of the hotel.

One rises to this position only after many years of training in the field. This is not an entry-level position, and it can only be attained with extensive experience. As one of the top posts in a hotel organization, the pay here is quite high and often augmented by bonuses.

There are assistantships and office positions available in this department. The assistantships require almost as much experience as the top post, and appointments to the top post are often made from the ranks of assistants. Right under the catering director are the chef-steward and wine steward, and, in some hotels, the banquet manager is partly responsible to the catering director for the food preparation and pricing of sales.

Chef-Steward

The chef-steward is in charge of the preparation of all food sold both in the dining rooms and through room service and banquets. He or she plans menus; purchases, prepares, and serves the food dishes; and supervises the various assistant chefs and other personnel in the department. The chef-steward usually is directly responsible to the catering manager. In some hotels, the chef is independent of the catering manager and is sometimes assisted by a steward who makes purchases and supervises the noncooking or baking employees of the food department.

Food items for hotels are usually purchased daily. It would be impossible to store all the fresh vegetables, fruits, bakery products, meats, and fish it takes to provide the thousands of meals served daily by some of the large hotels.

As the catering manager and chef are both interested in food costs and control, menus are generally planned according to availability and daily market quotations. In large operations, the saving of a fraction of a cent per dish can mean a good-sized profit. For this reason, the chef and catering manager try to base their menus on the best-priced seasonal items, where they can make cuts and save money without impairing the quality of the food. Working as closely as they do, it is generally difficult to make up menus more than a day or two in advance.

The specific duties of the chef are discussed in detail later in this chapter.

Liquor and Food Controls

Since the catering manager, the chef, and the wine steward must ensure that their respective departments show a profit, rigid food and liquor controls are observed. The costs of preparing meals and drinks are calculated to the smallest fraction. When correlated with similar labor, overhead, and hidden cost analyses, profit or loss per portion can be assessed. Many restaurants and hotel food departments show a loss because of inefficient food controls. Hidden costs and wastes that do not show up on general cost figures can result in inefficient and unprofitable operation at the end of a fiscal period.

All hotel operations use a checking system to control food and liquor orders. The systems vary with different hotels and types of employees, but some type of control is necessary to prevent loss of revenue caused by inefficient billing or fraud. Checking is also important in compiling food statistics for use in analysis of food operations, costs, and profits. Checkers, responsible to the accounting department, perform this control function.

Room Service

Room service can be a highly profitable food operation for a hotel if it is well promoted and efficiently managed. In smaller hotels, bellhops or regular dining room attendants provide room service. In medium-sized and large hotels, room service is run as a separate department.

There are many opportunities for employment here, including positions as waiters and waitresses, assistant waiters and waitresses, telephone order takers, assistant managers, and room service manager. The manager of this department is responsible for the efficient operation of the department; this includes the interviewing, disciplining, instructing, and discharging of the employees in room service.

In hotels where room service is provided as a separate service, the department is usually set up on a two-shift system, with the night shift eliminated. Occasionally, some hotels will stagger the day shifts so that service is provided until 1:00 or 2:00 A.M.

Room service positions can lead to positions of management in one of the dining rooms or the banquet department. Steps higher up the ladder are to positions as banquet head-waiter, catering manager, and eventually managerial work.

There are opportunities to enter the room service department as an apprentice waiter or waitress. Most hotels insist on experience for waiting in room service, but some will employ and train applicants without previous experience. Positions in this department may lead to that of head of the room service department and beyond.

Wine Steward

The sale of wines and beverages varies depending on location. In some areas, the sale of alcoholic beverages is forbidden; in others, local ordinances may differ from town to town. You will need to be aware of the local situation if you are interested in a position involving alcoholic beverages.

The wine steward generally has supervision of the wine and beverage departments in larger hotels. An expert in the field, this person supervises the placing of orders, the storage, and the issuance of wines and liquors for use by guests. The steward must be knowledgeable about vintages, the proper care of wines and liquors, and the history of the profession and its products. The wine steward also supervises the work of the employees of the department, interviewing, instructing, disciplining, and discharging employees as required. He or she is responsible for seeing that wines and liquors are on hand in sufficient quantity and quality to meet all guest demands, that they are ordered according to demand, and that the department shows a profit from sales.

The position of wine steward is a highly honored one in a hotel. It was originally handed down from generation to generation or granted only after many years of apprenticeship and experience as a wine steward's assistant. Today, promotion to this position is made from the ranks of assistant wine stewards or head bartenders. A great deal of specific experience is needed here, and it is gained only from years of work and training in this department.

Entry-level opportunities do exist in the food and liquor departments. Openings exist for apprentices in the kitchen; for assistants and student waiters in the dining rooms, the banquet service, and room service departments; and for assistant bartenders and assistants to the wine steward in the liquor department.

Experienced bartenders are in demand at many hotels. Bartenders fill drink orders either taken directly from patrons at the bar or through waiters and waitresses who place drink orders for dining room customers. Bartenders check identification of customers seated at the bar to ensure they meet the minimum age requirement for the purchase of alcohol. They must know a wide range of drink recipes and be able to mix drinks accurately, quickly, and without waste. Hotels with special house mixtures will train their bartenders in the mixing and serving of these drinks. Besides mixing and serving drinks, bartenders stock and prepare garnishes for drinks; maintain an adequate supply of ice, glasses, and other bar supplies; and keep the bar area clean for customers. They also may collect payment, operate the cash register, wash glassware and utensils, and serve food to customers seated at the bar.

Assisting the bartenders are the assistant bartenders, who chop ice, remove empty glasses or trash, bring in supplies, and set up ingredients for use by the bartender. From assistant bartender, the next promotion is to bartender or assistant to the wine steward. From bartender, one usually advances to head bartender and then to wine steward.

Most bartenders are required to have previous experience, but assistant bartenders who have had no previous experience may be considered for the job. There are numerous commercial bartenders' schools that offer courses of one to a few weeks at various tuition rates. If you consider a bartending school, it's wise to check its reputation with the institution where you want to work and be sure the training you receive would be looked on favorably for employment. As with other hotel positions, a high school education is the minimum requirement, but beginners in most large hotels are trained in the duties and business of wines and liquors by the wine steward or an assistant. Smaller hotels generally do not have openings for assistant bartenders, cellarmen, or wine stewards because of the small staff size.

Bartenders had median hourly earnings (including tips) of $7.21 in 2002. The middle 50 percent earned between $6.33 and $9.02; the lowest 10 percent earned less than $5.76; and the highest 10 percent earned more than $11.96 an hour. Like waiters and waitresses, bartenders employed in public bars may receive more than half of their earnings as tips. Service bartenders often are paid higher hourly wages to offset their lower tip earnings. The usual workweek is five or six days, eight hours a day.

The Kitchen

The preparation and serving of food is one of the most important and most skilled functions in any hotel, large or small. Since profit so frequently depends upon efficient and skillful operation of the food departments, the success or failure of a hotel depends in no small part upon the ability and experience of the chef-steward.

As stated earlier in this chapter, the best opportunities for entrance into the hotel field exist in the food department. Many hotel executives strongly recommend that the beginner consider this field before all others. In their opinion, knowledge of food is more important than almost anything else in the hotel business.

Most large hotels employ large staffs of cooks who specialize in the preparation of different kinds of foods. The executive chef, who is responsible for all of the hotel's kitchens, directs the cooking staff. The executive chef plans the menus, orders the food, supervises the other cooks, institutes the style of cooking, and originates the recipes. This person is responsible for the ordering of sufficient food to meet all guest needs, proper preparation and serving of the food, and the operation of the department at a profit.

A chef de cuisine reports to the executive chef and is responsible for the daily operations of a single kitchen. A sous chef, or sub chef, is the second-in-command and runs the kitchen in the absence of the chef. Chefs tend to be more highly skilled and better trained than cooks. Many chefs earn fame for themselves and their kitchens because of the quality and distinctive nature of the food they serve.

Other cooks in the kitchen may include a salad chef, cold meat chef, roast chef, sauce chef, dessert chef, and so on. There may also be butchers, bakers, and pastry chefs. The specialization will depend upon the size of the staff. In addition, there are helpers, assistants, and apprentices.

Many hotels have fine restaurants, and the executive chefs and head cooks who work in these establishments require many years of training and experience and an intense desire to cook. Some chefs and cooks may start their training in high school or post–high school vocational programs. Others may receive formal training through independent cooking schools, professional culinary institutes, or two- or four-year college degree programs in hospitality or culinary arts. In addition, some large hotels and restaurants operate their own training and job-placement programs for chefs and cooks. Most formal training programs require some form of apprenticeship, internship, or out-placement program that are jointly offered by the school and affiliated restaurants. Professional culinary institutes, industry associations, and trade unions also may sponsor formal apprenticeship programs. Many chefs are trained on the job, receiving real work experience and training from chef mentors in the restaurants where they work.

Training, Hours, and Earnings

People who have had courses in commercial food preparation may start in a cook or chef job without spending a lot of time in lower-skilled kitchen jobs. Their education might give them an advantage when looking for jobs in better restaurants. Some vocational programs in high schools might offer training, but employers usually prefer training given by trade schools, vocational centers, colleges, professional associations, or trade unions. Postsecondary courses range from a few months to two years or more. Degree-granting programs are open only to high school graduates. Chefs also may compete and test for certification as master chefs. Although certification is not required to enter the field, it can be a measure of accomplishment; it can also lead to further advancement and higher-paying positions. The U.S. Armed Forces are a good source of training and experience as well. See Appendix A for a list of schools and colleges that provide culinary training.

The hours of kitchen staff vary, depending on the hotel's dining policies. Wages of chefs, cooks, and food preparation workers vary greatly according to location and size of the hotel. Wages usually are highest in elegant hotels and in major metropolitan areas.

Median hourly earnings of chefs and head cooks in all areas were $13.43 in 2002. The middle 50 percent earned between $9.86 and $19.03; the lowest 10 percent earned less than $7.66; and the highest 10 percent earned more than $25.86 per hour. Those employed in the hotel industry earned an average of $17.03 per hour. Median hourly earnings of cooks in the hotel industry were $10.49.

Restaurant Operation

Restaurant operations in large hotels are carried out by managers who report to the catering manager. Each restaurant in the hotel is operated by the restaurant manager, whose duties include the interviewing, instructing, disciplining, and discharging of employees; keeping records; handling customers' complaints; sometimes preparing menus or making suggestions for menu items; and supervising all the various activities that are required to make the restaurant efficient and attractive.

In some smaller hotels, a restaurant manager may work very closely with the chef in preparing the menus and purchasing the food. A thorough knowledge of preparing, storing, and purchasing food, as well as food cost accounting, menu preparation, and checking, is helpful in this work. In addition, the manager must be familiar with sanitary practices and local regulations. He or she also supervises and assigns duties to employees, seeing that no favoritism is shown any particular member of the department.

Technology influences the jobs of restaurant managers in many ways, enhancing efficiency and productivity. Many hotels use computers to track orders, inventory, and the seating of patrons in restaurants. Point-of-service (POS) systems allow servers to key in a customer's order, either at the table using a handheld device or from a computer terminal in the dining room, and send the order to the kitchen instantaneously so preparation can begin. The same system totals and prints checks, functions as a cash register, connects to credit card authorizers, and tracks sales. To minimize food costs and spoilage, many managers use inventory-tracking software to compare the record of sales from the POS with a record of the current inventory. Computers also allow restaurant managers to keep track of employee schedules and paychecks more efficiently.

Many large national or regional hotel chains recruit restaurant management trainees from two- and four-year college hospitality management programs. Many chains prefer to hire people with degrees in restaurant and institutional food service management, but they often hire graduates with degrees in other fields who have demonstrated interest and aptitude. Waiters, waitresses, and chefs who demonstrate potential for handling increased responsibility sometimes advance to assistant manager or management trainee jobs. General managers need prior restaurant experience, usually as assistant managers.

A bachelor's degree in restaurant and food service management provides particularly strong preparation for a career in this occupation. A number of colleges and universities offer four-year programs in restaurant and hotel management or institutional food service management. For those not interested in pursuing a four-year degree, community and junior colleges, technical institutes, and other institutions offer programs in the field leading to an associate degree or other formal certification.

The certified Foodservice Management Professional (FMP) designation is a measure of professional achievement for food service managers. Although not a requirement for employment or advancement in the occupation, voluntary certification provides recognition of professional competence, particularly for managers who acquired their skills largely on the job. The National Restaurant Association Educational Foundation awards the FMP designation to managers who achieve a qualifying score on a written examination, complete a series of courses that cover a range of food service management topics, and meet standards of work experience in the field.

Willingness to relocate often is essential for advancement to positions with greater responsibility. Managers typically advance to larger establishments or regional management positions within large chains.

The restaurant manager is assisted by a captain. In addition to managerial duties, the captain assists in leading diners to tables, assigning waiters to stations, and ensuring that the guests are seated at wait stations in rotation so that work is distributed evenly among the wait staff.

In addition to the restaurant manager and captain, hotel restaurants employ waiters and waitresses, assistant waiters and waitresses, cashiers, and other assistants. Besides taking guest orders and serving food and liquor to tables, the wait staff also sets tables, sometimes collects payment, makes out checks, arranges setups, helps bus tables when busy, and performs other chores.

Though most hotels employ only men and women who have had table service experience in other hotels or restaurants, many hotels have begun training their assistant waiters and waitresses for promotion as positions become available. Some hotels are even engaging persons with no previous wait experience in order to train them in the hotel's own system.

In this field of hotel operation, hours of work and earnings vary greatly. Hours depend upon local hours of service, working conditions, and many other factors. Earnings are based on tips as well as salaries, and meals are usually provided.

Housekeeping Department

Much of the reputation of a hotel lies in the hands of its housekeeper and the housekeeping staff. The most important thing sought by the average hotel guest is a clean, neat, attractive, cheerful, comfortable room. The appearance of the public areas is also important to guests. An inefficient housekeeper can ruin a hotel's reputation almost overnight. A successful hotel must maintain the highest housekeeping standards.

The executive or head housekeeper is chief of the housekeeping department. It is this person's responsibility to see that halls, rooms, and furnishings are kept clean and attractive. In hotels with large housekeeping staffs, the executive housekeeper has additional duties, including assisting in or making purchases of supplies for the department; interviewing, disciplining, instructing, and discharging employees in the department; keeping employee and housekeeping records; making regular reports to the manager regarding conditions, repairs, improvements, employee problems, expenditures, and suggestions; keeping inventories; and making out the department payroll. In some instances a skilled housekeeper will be involved in the creation of new schemes of interior decoration.

In large hotels, the housekeeping staff may include linen room attendants, assistant housekeepers, floor supervisors, housekeepers, furniture polishers, wall and window washers, seamstresses, upholsterers, painters, cabinetmakers, and others skilled in housekeeping repair and maintenance.

Promotion to executive housekeeper is usually made from the housekeeping staff or by employing persons with experience from other hotels. Frequently, inexperienced persons are employed as assistants to floor supervisors and given training in their work. While previous training and experience are usually preferred for executive work in the housekeeping department, many have risen to top positions here from lesser jobs. Many high schools and vocational schools offer training courses for housekeeping jobs. Courses in housekeeping are also part of certain two- and four-year programs offered by many colleges.

A small number of cleaning supervisors and managers are members of the International Executive Housekeepers Association. This association offers two kinds of certification programs: Certified Executive Housekeeper (CEH) and Registered Executive Housekeeper (REH). The CEH designation is offered to those with a high school education, while the REH designation is offered to those who have a four-year college degree. Both designations are earned by attending courses and passing exams, and both must be renewed every two years to ensure that workers keep abreast of new cleaning methods. Those with the REH designation usually oversee the cleaning services of hotels, casinos, and other large institutions that rely on well-trained experts for their housekeeping needs.

Openings as maid, housekeeper, supervisor, and other jobs in the housekeeping department are available to persons with little or no experience, and application should be made to the executive housekeeper.

Although lesser jobs in the housekeeping field often do not pay well, they are advantageous in that they are available to persons with little or no previous experience. To persons with the ambition and ability to succeed, these jobs offer opportunity to advance, since the rate of turnover in the housekeeping field is rather high.

Earnings of executive housekeepers average $28,471 a year in small hotels (fewer than 150 rooms) to $66,825 a year in large hotels (more than 800 rooms). In some hotels, executive housekeepers earn much more. Meals and lodging are quite often given in addition to cash earnings. (For more information, go online to the Hospitality Career Network, http://hospitalitycareernet.com/careerresources/lodgprop.asp.)

Additional Positions

There are many other hotel jobs in addition to those specialized trades we have described. Although important to the hotel's operation, these other jobs are not hotel trades as such and do not require specific hotel experience. Among these other departments are engineering, telephone, laundry, valet, medical, and dental.

The engineering department operates the hotel's water, heat, and other physical facilities. In a large hotel, the engineering department will include boiler room attendants, carpenters, electricians, engine room attendants, maintenance engineers, plumbers, painters, compression workers, and others. Required experience for these positions depends upon the job to be filled. Hotel experience is not a prime factor in employment; rather, a background in a specific trade is more important than previous hotel work. Some positions require appropriate state licensing. Hours and wages vary with the nature of the work and the size of the hotel. In addition, many workers in skilled trades are members of labor unions.

Many hotels also employ telephone operators, laundry help, and valets (pressing and tailoring). Inquiries concerning openings, hours, and remuneration should be made to the personnel director.

In some large hotels, medical and dental services are available on the premises for the convenience of guests and for emergencies among the employees. These openings are filled from regular medical and dental channels. Medical or dental clinics can use nurses, receptionists, and secretaries. Make inquiries directly at the clinic or office.

In addition, there are numerous secretarial, clerical, computer operating, reception, and other jobs in hotels. Inquiries for these should be made at the human resources office.

Some Final Words

Remember, career decisions are often difficult. Talk to others working in the field. Get all of the facts before making a choice. Choosing your career should be a positive and exciting experience! Paul Grossinger, of Grossinger's, the famous New York state resort hotel, once said of a career in the hospitality field:

> The hotel industry today is certainly one to challenge the ability of any young person. Certainly no other business gives a person the opportunity of meeting so many various kinds of people, and no other business displays the human element as graphically.
>
> A hotel is a world unto its own. We house and we feed people and also, in many instances, entertain them. We provide stopping areas, some as modest as a candy store, others as lavish as a series

of shops operated by the best-known names in the retail world. Certainly, an industry such as this is one to excite the imagination of the young. Most hotel people find that their business and social lives are greatly integrated. Most of us think that this is a benefit.

Financial gains in this industry are to the capable. Certainly, the basic concept of salary and wages in a hotel have gone up tremendously. Opportunity lies within the grasp of those who truly seek it.

Personally, I would not think of making my living in any other manner.

Appendix A

Educational Programs in Hotel and Hospitality Management

The following is a list of colleges and universities that offer four-year (bachelor's degree) programs or two-year (associate's degree) programs in hotel, restaurant, and institutional management or food service administration. A number of schools offer a master's degree either in business administration or in hotel, restaurant, and institutional management; these programs are marked with the letter M to the right of their listing.

Requests for additional information should be directed to the admissions office or the hotel and/or hospitality management program at each school.

Please note that many of the schools offer programs at more than one location or in several areas of hospitality management. Check the websites for the most complete information available about schools and programs in which you are interested.

Four-Year Programs

Alabama

Auburn University
Hotel Restaurant Management and Tourism Program
College of Human Sciences
210 Spindle Hall
Auburn, AL 36849
www.humsci.auburn.edu

Tuskegee University
Hospitality Management Program
College of Business and Information Science
Tuskegee, AL 36088
www.tuskegee.edu

University of Alabama
Restaurant and Hospitality Management Program
College of Human Environmental Sciences
Tuscaloosa, AL 35487
www.ches.ua.edu

Alaska

University of Alaska–Anchorage
Hospitality and Restaurant Management Program
Community and Technical College
Anchorage, AK 99508
www.uaa.alaska.edu

Arizona

Northern Arizona University
School of Hotel and Restaurant Management
Box 5638
Flagstaff, AZ 86011
www.nau.edu

Arkansas

Arkansas Tech University
Hospitality Administration Program
Williamson Hall, Rm. 101
1509 N. Boulder Ave.
Russellville, AR 72801
www.atu.edu

California

Alliant International University–San Diego
Hotel, Restaurant, and Tourism Management
United States International College of Business
6160 Cornerstone Ct. East
San Diego, CA 92121
www.alliant.edu/usicb

California State Polytechnic University–Pomona
Collins School of Hospitality Management
3801 W. Temple Ave., #79B
Pomona, CA 91710
http://www.csupomona.edu

San Francisco State University
Hospitality Management Department
College of Business
1600 Holloway Ave.
San Francisco, CA 94132
http://www.sfsu.edu

San Jose State University
Hospitality Management
College of Applied Sciences and Arts
MacQuarrie Hall 517
San Jose, CA 95192
www.hospitality.sjsu.edu

University of San Francisco
Hospitality Industry Management
2130 Fulton St.
San Francisco, CA 94117
www.usfca.edu

Colorado

Colorado State University
Restaurant and Resort Management Program
College of Applied Human Sciences
Ft. Collins, CO 80523
www.cahs.colostate.edu

Fort Lewis College
Tourism and Resort Management
School of Business Administration
100 Rim Dr.
Durango, CO 81301
www.fortlewis.edu

Johnson & Wales University
The Hospitality College
7150 Montview Blvd.
Denver, CO 80220
www.jwu.edu

Metropolitan State College of Denver
Hospitality, Meeting, Travel Administration
P.O. Box 173362
Plaza Bldg. 124, Campus Box 60
Denver, CO 80204
www.mscd.edu

University of Denver
Hotel, Restaurant, and Tourism Management
Daniels College of Business
102 S. University Blvd.
Denver, CO 80208
www.daniels.du.edu

Connecticut

University of New Haven (M)
School of Hospitality and Tourism
300 Boston Post Rd.
West Haven, CT 06516
www.newhaven.edu

Delaware

Delaware State University
Hospitality and Tourism Management
School of Management
1200 DuPont Hwy.
Dover, DE 19901
www.dsc.edu

University of Delaware (M)
Hotel, Restaurant, and Institutional Management
College of Human Services, Education, and Public Policy
Newark, DE 19716
www.udel.edu

District of Columbia

Howard University
Hospitality Management Program
School of Business
2400 6th St. NW
Washington, DC 20059
www.howard.edu

Florida

Bethune-Cookman College
Hospitality Management Program
640 Dr. Mary McLeod Bethune Blvd.
Daytona Beach, FL 32141
www.bethune.cookman.edu

Florida International University (M)
School of Hospitality and Tourism Management
Biscayne Bay Campus
North Miami, FL 33181
http://hospitality.fiu.edu

Florida Metropolitan University
Hospitality Management Program
Pompano Beach Campus
225 N. Federal Hwy.
Pompano Beach, FL 33062
www.fmu.edu

Florida Southern College
Hotel/Resort Management
111 Lake Hollingsworth Dr.
Lakeland, FL 33801
www.flsouthern.edu

Florida State University (M)
Dedman School of Hospitality
College of Business
1 Champions Way, Ste. 4100
Tallahassee, FL 32306
www.fsu.edu

Johnson & Wales University
The Hospitality College
1701 NE 127 St.
North Miami, FL 33181
www.jwu.edu

Lynn University
Hospitality Management
3601 N. Military Trail
Boca Raton, FL 33431
www.lynn.edu

Saint Leo University
International Hospitality and Tourism Management
33701 State Road 52
Saint Leo, FL 33574
www.saintleo.edu

Schiller International University (M)
International Hotel and Tourism Management
453 Edgewater Dr.
Dunedin, FL 34698
www.schiller.edu

St. Thomas University
Tourism and Hospitality Management
16401 NW 37th Ave.
Miami Gardens, FL 33054
www.stu.edu

University of Central Florida
Rosen College of Hospitality Management
9907 Universal Blvd.
Orlando, FL 32819
www.ucf.edu

Webber International University
Hospitality Business Management
1201 N. Scenic Hwy.
Babson Park, FL 33827
www.webber.edu

Georgia

Georgia Southern University
Hotel and Restaurant Management
Statesboro, GA 30458
www.georgiasouthern.edu

Georgia State University
Hospitality Administration
J. Mack Robinson College of Business
35 Broad St. NW
Atlanta, GA 30303
www.gsu.edu

Morris Brown College
Hospitality Administration
643 Martin Luther King Jr. Dr.
Atlanta, GA 30314
www.morrisbrown.edu

Hawaii

Brigham Young University–Hawaii
Hospitality and Tourism Program
55-220 Kulanui St.
Laie, HI 96762
www.byuh.edu

Hawaii Pacific University
Travel Industry Management
College of Business Administration
1164 Bishop St.
Honolulu, HI 96813
www.hpu.edu

University of Hawaii–Manoa (M)
School of Travel Industry Management
George Hall 346
2600 Campus Rd.
Honolulu, HI 96822
www.hawaii.edu

Illinois

Kendall College
Hospitality Management
900 N. Branch St.
Chicago, IL 60622
www.kendall.edu

Northern Illinois University
Hospitality Administration
College of Health and Human Sciences
DeKalb, IL 60115
www.niu.edu

Robert Morris College
Hospitality Management
School of Business Administration
401 S. State St.
Chicago, IL 60605
www.robertmorris.edu

Roosevelt University (M)
School of Hospitality and Tourism Management
430 S. Michigan Ave.
Chicago, IL 60605
www.roosevelt.edu

Southern Illinois University
Hospitality and Tourism Management
Department of Animal Science, Food, and Nutrition
Mail Code 4417
Carbondale, IL 62901
www.siu.edu

University of Illinois (M)
Hospitality Management
Department of Food Science and Human Nutrition
260 Bevier Hall
905 S. Goodwin
Urbana, IL 61801
www.uiuc.edu

Indiana

Purdue University (M)
Department of Hospitality and Tourism Management
West Lafayette, IN 47907
www.cfs.purdue.edu

Iowa

Iowa State University (M)
Hotel, Restaurant, and Institution Management
31 MacKay Hall
Ames, IA 50011
www.iastate.edu

Kansas

Kansas State University
Hotel and Restaurant Management
College of Human Ecology
Manhattan, KS 66506
www.k-state.edu

Kentucky

Morehead State University
Hotel, Restaurant, and Institutional Management
Department of Agricultural and Human Sciences
325 Reed Hall
Morehead, KY 40351
www.morehead-st.edu

Transylvania University
Hotel, Restaurant, and Tourism Administration
300 N. Broadway
Lexington, KY 40508
www.transy.edu

University of Kentucky
Hospitality Management and Tourism
College of Agriculture
Erikson Hall
Lexington, KY 40506
www.uky.edu

Western Kentucky University
Hotel, Restaurant, and Tourism Management
Department of Consumer and Family Sciences
One Big Red Way
Bowling Green, KY 42101
www.wku.edu

Louisiana

University of Louisiana–Lafayette
Hospitality Management
College of Applied Life Sciences
611 McKinley Dr.
Lafayette, LA 70504
www.louisiana.edu

University of New Orleans (M)
School of Hotel, Restaurant, and Tourism Administration
College of Business Administration
2000 Lakeshore Dr.
New Orleans, LA 70148
www.uno.edu

Maine

Thomas College
Hotel and Restaurant Management
180 W. River Rd.
Waterville, ME 04901
www.thomas.edu

Maryland

Baltimore International College
Hospitality Management
Commerce Exchange
17 Commerce St.
Baltimore, MD 21202
www.bic.edu

Morgan State University
Hotel, Restaurant, and Hospitality Management
Department of Human Ecology
1700 E. Cold Springs La.
Baltimore, MD 21251
www.morgan.edu

University of Maryland–Eastern Shore
Hotel and Restaurant Management
School of Business and Technology
11868 Academic Oval
Princess Anne, MD 21853
www.umes.edu

Massachusetts

Boston University
School of Hospitality Administration
808 Commonwealth Ave.
Boston, MA 02215
www.bu.edu

Lasell College
Hospitality Management
1844 Commonwealth Ave.
Newton, MA 02466
www.lasell.edu

Mount Ida College
Hotel and Tourism Management
777 Dedham St.
Newton, MA 02459
www.mountida.edu

Newbury College
Saunders School of Hotel and Restaurant Management
129 Fisher Ave.
Brookline, MA 02445
www.newbury.edu

University of Massachusetts–Amherst (M)
Hospitality and Tourism Management
Isenberg School of Management
107 Flint Lab
90 Campus Way
Amherst, MA 01003
www.umass.edu

Michigan

Central Michigan University (M)
Hospitality and Tourism Administration
Mt. Pleasant, MI 48859
www.cmich.edu

Ferris State University
Hotel Management
1319 Cramer Circle
Big Rapids, MI 49307
www.ferris.edu

Grand Valley State University
Hospitality and Tourism Management
1 Campus Dr.
Allendale, MI 49401
www.gvsu.edu

Michigan State University (M)
School of Hospitality Business
232 Eppley Center
East Lansing, MI 48824
www.msu.edu

Northern Michigan University
Hospitality Management
School of Technology and Applied Sciences
1401 Presque Isle Ave.
Marquette, MI 49855
www.nmu.edu

Northwood University
Hotel, Restaurant, and Resort Management
4000 Whiting Dr.
Midland, MI 48640
www.northwood.edu

Siena Heights College
Hotel, Restaurant, and Institutional Management
Department of Business and Management
1247 E. Siena Heights Dr.
Adrian, MI 49221
www.sienahts.edu

Minnesota

Southwest Minnesota State University
Hotel, Restaurant, and Institutional Management
Department of Business and Public Affairs
1501 State St.
Marshall, MN 56258
www.southwestmsu.edu

University of Minnesota–Crookston
Hotel, Restaurant, and Institutional Management
Department of Business
2900 University Ave.
Crookston, MN 56716
www.crk.umn.edu

Mississippi

University of Southern Mississippi
Tourism Management
Department of Business
Hattiesburg, MS 39406
www.usm.edu

Missouri

College of the Ozarks
Hotel and Restaurant Management
Division of Human and Social Sciences
P.O. Box 17
Point Lookout, MO 65726
www.cofo.edu

Southwest Missouri State University
Hospitality and Restaurant Administration
Department of Consumer and Family Studies
901 S. National Ave.
Springfield, MO 65804
www.smsu.edu

University of Missouri–Columbia
Hotel and Restaurant Management Program
108 Eckles Hall
Columbia, MO 65211
www.missouri.edu

Nebraska

University of Nebraska–Lincoln
Foodservice Administration
Department of Nutritional Science and Dietetics
Lincoln, NE 68583
www.unl.edu

Nevada

Sierra Nevada College–Lake Tahoe
Hospitality and Tourism Management
Department of Management
999 Tahoe Blvd.
Incline Village, NV 89451
www.sierranevada.edu

University of Nevada–Las Vegas (M)
Harrah College of Hotel Administration
4505 Maryland Pkwy.
Box 456013
Las Vegas, NV 89154
www.unlv.edu

New Hampshire

University of New Hampshire
Hospitality Management
Whittemore School of Business and Economics
Durham, NH 03824
www.unh.edu

New Jersey

Fairleigh Dickinson University (M)
Hotel and Restaurant Management
International School of Hospitality and Tourism Management
285 Madison Ave.
Madison, NJ 07940
www.fdu.edu

New York

Cornell University (M)
School of Hotel Administration
Ithaca, NY 14853
www.cornell.edu

New York Institute of Technology
Hospitality Management
School of Education and Professional Services
1855 Broadway
New York, NY 10023
www.nyit.edu

New York University (M)
Hospitality, Tourism, and Travel Administration
22 Washington Sq. North
New York, NY 10003
www.nyu.edu

Niagara University (M)
College of Hospitality and Tourism Management
Niagara, NY 14109
www.niagara.edu

Rochester Institute of Technology (M)
Hotel and Resort Management
1 Lomb Memorial Dr.
Rochester, NY 14623
www.rit.edu

State University of New York–Oneonta
Food Service and Restaurant Administration
Ravine Pkwy.
Oneonta, NY 13820
www.oneonta.edu

State University of New York–Plattsburgh (Plattsburgh State)
Hotel, Restaurant, and Tourism Management
Plattsburgh, NY 12901
www.plattsburgh.edu

Syracuse University
Nutrition and Hospitality Management
College of Human Services and Health Professions
034 Slocum Hall
Syracuse, NY 13244
www.syr.edu

North Carolina

East Carolina University (M)
Nutrition and Hospitality Management
College of Human Ecology
Rivers Bldg.
Greenville, NC 27858
www.ecu.edu

Johnson & Wales University
The Hospitality College
801 W. Trade St.
Charlotte, NC 28202
www.jwu.edu

North Carolina Central University
Hospitality and Tourism Administration
School of Business
1801 Fayetteville St.
Durham, NC 27707
www.nccu.edu

North Dakota

North Dakota State University
Hospitality and Tourism Management
College of Human Development and Education
Evelyn Morrow Lebedeff Hall 178
Fargo, ND 58105
www.ndsu.edu

Ohio

Ashland University
Hotel and Restaurant Management
College of Business and Economics
401 College Ave.
Ashland, OH 44805
www.ashland.edu

Kent State University
Hospitality Management
College of Fine and Professional Arts
Kent, OH 44242
www.kent.edu

Tiffin University
Hospitality and Tourism Management
School of Business
Tiffin, OH 44883
www.tiffin.edu

Youngstown State University
Hospitality Management Program
Department of Human Ecology
Youngstown, OH 44555
www.ysu.edu

Oklahoma

University of Central Oklahoma
Hotel and Foodservice Administration
College of Business Administration
100 N. University Dr.
Edmond, OK 73034
www.ucok.edu

Oregon

Oregon State University
Food Science and Technology
Corvallis, OR 97331
www.oregonstate.edu

Pennsylvania

Cheyney University
Hotel, Restaurant, and Institutional Management
Department of Professional Services
1837 University Circle
P.O. Box 200
Cheyney, PA 19319
www.cheney.edu

Drexel University
Hospitality Management
Philadelphia, PA 19104
www.drexel.edu

East Stroudsburg University
Hotel, Restaurant, and Tourism Management
School of Professional Studies
200 Prospect St.
East Stroudsburg, PA 18301
www.esu.edu

Indiana University of Pennsylvania
Hospitality Management
Ackerman Hall, Rm. 10
911 South Dr.
Indiana, PA 25705
www.iup.edu

Marywood University
Hospitality Management
Business and Managerial Science Department
2300 Adams Ave.
Scranton, PA 18509
www.marywood.edu

Mercyhurst College
Hotel, Restaurant, and Institutional Management
501 East 38th St.
Erie, PA 16546
www.mercyhurst.edu

Pennsylvania State University (M)
Hotel, Restaurant, and Institutional Management
College of Health and Human Development
State College, PA 16802
www.psu.edu

Widener University (M)
School of Hospitality Management
1 University Pl.
Chester, PA 19013
www.widener.edu

Rhode Island

Johnson & Wales University (M)
The Hospitality College
Providence, RI 02903
www.jwu.edu

South Carolina

Johnson & Wales University
The Hospitality College
701 E. Bay St.
Charleston, SC 29403
www.jwu.edu

University of South Carolina (M)
School of Hotel, Restaurant, and Tourism Management
Columbia, SC 29208
www.sc.edu

South Dakota

Black Hills State University
Tourism and Hospitality Management
College of Business and Technology
1200 University St., Unit 9502
Spearfish, SD 57799
www.bhsu.edu

South Dakota State University
Hotel and Foodservice Management
College of Family and Consumer Sciences
Brookings, SD 57007
www.sdstate.edu

Tennessee

Belmont University
Hospitality, Travel, and Tourism
College of Business
1900 Belmont Blvd.
Nashville, TN 37212
www.belmont.edu

Tennessee State University
Hospitality and Tourism Administration
College of Business
3500 John A. Merritt Blvd.
Nashville, TN 37209
www.tnstate.edu

University of Tennessee (M)
Hotel and Restaurant Administration Program
Department of Consumer Services Management
110 Jessie Harris Bldg.
1215 W. Cumberland Ave.
Knoxville, TN 37996
www.utk.edu

Texas

Stephen F. Austin State University
Hospitality Administration
Department of Human Sciences
Box 13014 SFA Station
Nacogdoches, TX 75962
www.sfasu.edu

Texas Tech University (M)
Restaurant, Hotel, and Institutional Management
Nutrition, Hospitality, and Retailing Department
Box 41162
Lubbock, TX 79409
www.ttu.edu

University of Houston (M)
Hilton College of Hotel and Restaurant Management
4800 Calhoun Rd.
Houston, TX 77204
www.uh.edu

University of North Texas (M)
Hospitality Management
School of Merchandising and Hospitality Management
P.O. Box 311277
Denton, TX 76203
www.unt.edu

Vermont

Champlain College
Hospitality Industry Management
163 S. Willard St.
Burlington, VT 05401
www.champlain.edu

Johnson State College
Hospitality and Tourism Management
337 College Hill
Johnson, VT 05656
www.johnsonstatecollege.edu

Virginia

James Madison University
Hospitality and Tourism Management
College of Business
MSC 0205
Harrisonburg, VA 22807
www.jmu.edu

Johnson & Wales University
Hospitality Department
2428 Almeda Ave., Ste. 316
Norfolk, VA 23513
www.jwu.edu

Norfolk State University
Tourism and Hospitality Department
700 Park Ave.
Norfolk, VA 23504
www.nsu.edu

Virginia Polytechnic Institute and State University (M)
(Virginia Tech)
Hospitality and Tourism Management
362 Wallace Hall (0429)
Blacksburg, VA 24061
www.vt.edu

Washington

Washington State University
School of Hospitality Business Management
Todd Addition 470
P.O. Box 644742
Pullman, WA 99164
www.wsu.edu

West Virginia

Concord University
Hospitality Management
Vermillion St.
P.O. Box 1000
Athens, WV 24712
www.concord.wvnet.edu

Davis & Elkins College
Hospitality Management
Business Administration and Economics Department
100 Campus Dr.
Elkins, WV 26241
www.davisandelkins.com

Wisconsin

University of Wisconsin–Stout (M)
Hotel, Restaurant, and Tourism Management
Menomonie, WI 54751
www.uwstout.edu

Two-Year Programs

Alabama

James H. Faulkner State Community College
Hospitality and Tourism Management Center
3301 Gulf Shores Pkwy.
Gulf Shores, AL 36542
www.faulkner.cc.al.us

Jefferson State Community College
Hospitality Management
Center for Professional, Career, and Technical Education
Fitzgerald Student Center, Rm. 100-C
2601 Carson Rd.
Birmingham, AL 35215
www.jeffstateonline.com

Arizona

Central Arizona College
Hotel and Restaurant Management Program
Business Division
8470 N. Overfield Rd.
Coolidge, AZ 85228
www.centralaz.edu

Pima Community College
Hotel and Restaurant Management
4905 E. Broadway Blvd.
Tucson, AZ 85709
www.pima.edu

Scottsdale Community College
Hospitality, Tourism, and Culinary Arts Division
9000 E. Chaparral Rd.
Scottsdale, AZ 85256
www.sc.maricopa.edu

Arkansas

North Arkansas College
Restaurant Management Program
1515 Pioneer Dr.
Harrison, AR 72601
www.northark.edu

California

American River College
Culinary Arts and Hospitality Management
4700 College Oak Blvd.
Sacramento, CA 95841
www.arc.losrios.edu

Bakersfield College
Hotel/Motel Management Program
1801 Panorama Dr.
Bakersfield, CA 93305
www.bc.cc.ca.us

California Culinary Academy
Hospitality and Restaurant Management Program
625 Polk St.
San Francisco, CA 94102
www.baychef.com

City College of San Francisco
Hotel and Restaurant Department
50 Phelan Ave.
San Francisco, CA 94112
www.ccsf.edu

College of the Canyons
Hotel/Restaurant Management Program
26455 Rockwell Canyon Rd.
Santa Clarita, CA 91355
www.canyons.edu

Cypress College
Hotel, Restaurant, and Culinary Arts Management
Bldg. Tech Ed I, 2nd Fl.
9200 Valley View St.
Cypress, CA 90630
www.cypresscollege.edu

Heald College
Hospitality and Tourism Program
255 W. Bullard Ave.
Fresno, CA 93704
www.heald.edu

Lake Tahoe Community College
Hotel and Restaurant Management Program
1 College Dr.
South Lake Tahoe, CA 96150
www.ltcc.cc.ca.us

Long Beach City College
Hospitality, Tourism, Restaurant, and Catering Programs
4901 E. Carson St.
Long Beach, CA 90808
www.lbcc.edu

Mira Costa College
Hospitality, Tourism, and Restaurant Programs
1 Barnard Dr.
Oceanside, CA 92056
www.miracosta.cc.ca.us

Mission College
Hospitality Management
3000 Mission College Blvd.
Santa Clara, CA 95054
www.missioncollege.org

Monterey Peninsula College
Hospitality Department
Life Sciences Division
980 Fremont St.
Monterey, CA 93940
www.mpc.edu

Mt. San Antonio College
Hospitality and Restaurant Management Program
Business and Economic Development Division
1100 N. Grand Ave.
Walnut, CA 91789
www.mtsac.edu

Orange Coast College
Hotel and Food Service Management Programs
Consumer and Health Sciences Division
2701 Fairview Rd.
Costa Mesa, CA 92626
www.orangecoastcollege.edu

San Diego Mesa College
Hotel/Motel Management Program and Food Service Occupations
7250 Mesa College Dr.
San Diego, CA 92111
www.sdmesa.sdccd.cc.ca.us

Santa Barbara City College
School of Culinary Arts and Hotel Management
721 Cliff Dr.
Santa Barbara, CA 93109
www.sbcc.cc.ca.us

Santa Rosa Junior College
CulinaryArts Program
1501 Mendocino Ave.
Santa Rosa, CA 95401
www.santarosa.edu

Colorado

Colorado Mountain College
Alpine Campus
Resort Management Program
1330 Bob Adams Dr.
Steamboat Springs, CO 80487
www.coloradomtn.edu

Front Range Community College
Hospitality/Food Management Program
3645 W. 112th Ave.
Westminster, CO 80031
http://frcc.cc.co.us

Connecticut

Briarwood College
Hotel and Restaurant Management
2279 Mount Vernon Rd.
Southington, CT 06489
www.briarwood.edu

Manchester Community College
Hotel-Tourism Management
Great Path
Manchester, CT 06045
www.mcc.commnet.edu

Norwalk Community-Technical College
Hospitality/Culinary Arts Program
188 Richards Ave.
Norwalk, CT 06854
www.ncc.commnet.edu

Three Rivers Community College
Hospitality Program
7 Mahan Dr.
Norwich, CT 06360
www.trcc.commnet.edu

Delaware

Delaware Tech
Hotel, Restaurant, and Institutional Management
Department of Business Administration
Route 18
P.O. Box 610
Georgetown, DE 19947
www.dtcc.edu

Florida

Brevard Community College
Hospitality Management Program
1519 Clearlake Rd.
Cocoa, FL 32922
www.brevard.cc.fl.us

Broward Community College
Hospitality and Tourism Management
111 E. Los Olas Blvd.
Ft. Lauderdale, FL 33301
www.broward.edu

Daytona Beach Community College
Hospitality Management
1200 W. International Speedway Blvd.
Daytona Beach, FL 32114
www.dbcc.cc.fl.us

Florida Community College–Jacksonville
Culinary Arts and Hospitality Program
501 W. State St.
Jacksonville, FL 32202
www.fccj.org

Hillsborough Community College
Hospitality Management Program
Dale Mabry Campus
P.O. Box 30030
Tampa, FL 33630
www.hccfl.edu

Keiser College of Technology
Hospitality Management Program
1500 NW 49th St.
Ft. Lauderdale, FL 33309
www.keisercollege.edu

Keiser College of Technology
Hospitality Services Program
900 S. Babcock St.
Melbourne, FL 32901
www.keisercollege.edu

Miami Dade College
Hospitality and Tourism Management
Homestead Campus
500 College Terrace
Homestead, FL 33030
www.mdc.edu

Palm Beach Community College
Culinary/Hospitality Program
4200 S. Congress Ave.
Lake Worth, FL 33461
www.pbcc.edu

Pensacola Junior College
Culinary and Hospitality Management
1000 College Blvd.
Pensacola, FL 32504
www.pjc.cc.fl.us

South Florida Community College
Hospitality and Tourism Management Program
600 W. College Dr.
Avon Park, FL 33825
www.sfcc.cc.fl.us

Valencia Community College
Hospitality and Tourism Management
P.O. Box 3028
Orlando, FL 32802
www.vcc.fl.us

Georgia

Georgia Highlands College (formerly Floyd College)
Hotel, Restaurant, and Travel Management
P.O. Box 1864
Rome, GA 30162
www.highlands.edu

Gwinnett Technical College
Hotel, Restaurant, Tourism Management
P.O. Box 1505
1250 Atkinson Rd.
Lawrenceville, GA 30246
www.gwinnetttechnicalcollege.com

Hawaii

Kapi'olani Community College
4303 Diamond Head Road
Honolulu, HI 96816
www.kcc.hawaii.edu

Kaua'i Community College
Hospitality Services and Hotel Operations Programs
3-1901 Kaumualii Hwy.
Lihue, Hi 96766
www.kauai.hawaii.edu

Idaho

College of Southern Idaho
Hospitality Management
315 Falls Ave.
P.O. Box 1238
Twin Falls, ID 83303
www.csi.edu

North Idaho College
Culinary Arts Program
1000 W. Garden Ave.
Coeur d'Alene, ID 83814
www.nic.edu

Illinois

Black Hawk College
Travel, Tourism, and Hospitality Program
6600 34th Ave.
Moline, IL 61275
www.bhc.edu

City Colleges of Chicago
Hospitality/Travel Programs
30 E. Lake St.
Chicago, IL 60601
www.ccc.edu

College of DuPage
Hotel/Motel Management Program
425 Fawell Blvd.
Glen Ellyn, IL 60137
www.cod.edu

The Cooking and Hospitality Institute of Chicago
361 W. Chestnut
Chicago, IL 60610
www.chic.edu

Elgin Community College
Hotel Management
1700 Spartan Dr.
Elgin, IL 60123
www.elgin.edu

Harper College
Hospitality Management Program
1200 W. Algonquin Rd.
Palatine, IL 60067
www.harpercollege.edu

Joliet Junior College
Culinary Arts Program
1216 Houbolt Rd.
Joliet, IL 60431
www.jjc.edu

Kendall College
Culinary Arts/Hospitality Management Programs
900 N. Branch St.
Chicago, IL 60622
www.kendall.edu

Lincoln Land Community College
Hotel/Motel Management
Department of Business Administration and Public Service
5250 Shepherd Rd.
Box 19256
Springfield, IL 62794
www.llcc.cc.il.us

MacCormac College
Hotel and Restaurant Management Program
29 E. Madison St.
Chicago, IL 60602
www.maccormac.edu

Moraine Valley Community College
Restaurant/Hotel Management
10900 S. 88th Ave.
Palos Hills, IL 60465
www.morainevalley.edu

Northwestern Business College
Hospitality Tourism Management
9700 W. Higgins Rd.
Rosemount, IL 60018
www.northwesternbc.edu

Triton College
Hotel/Motel Management
2000 Fifth Ave.
River Grove, IL 60171
www.triton.edu

Indiana

Indiana University—Purdue University–Ft. Wayne
Hotel, Restaurant, and Tourism Management Program
2101 E. Coliseum Blvd.
Ft. Wayne, IN 46805
www.ipfw.edu

Indiana University—Purdue University–Indianapolis
Tourism, Conventions, and Event Management
Cavanaugh Hall, Rm. 129
425 University Blvd.
Indianapolis, IN 46202
www.iupui.edu

Ivy Tech College–Central Indiana
Hospitality Administration Program
1 W. 26th St.
Indianapolis, IN 46208
www.culinaryschools.com

Purdue University
Hospitality and Tourism Management
College of Consumer and Family Sciences
700 W. State St.
West Lafayette, IN 47907
www.purdue.edu

Vincennes University
Hotel Management Program
Division of Business and Public Service
1002 N. First St.
Vincennes, IN 47591
www.vinu.edu

Iowa

Des Moines Area Community College
Hotel and Restaurant Management
2006 S. Ankeny Blvd.
Ankeny, IA 50021
www.dmacc.cc.ia.us

Iowa Lakes Community College
Hotel and Restaurant Management
19 S. 7th St.
Estherville, IA 51334
www.iowalakes.edu

Iowa Western Community College
Lodging and Hospitality Management
Council Bluffs, IA 51502
www.iwcc.cc.ia.us

Kirkwood Community College
Lodging and Restaurant Management Programs
Business and Information Technology Department
6301 Kirkwood Blvd. SW
Cedar Rapids, IA 52404
www.kirkwood.edu

Kansas

Cowley County Community College
Hotel and Restaurant Management
125 S. Second
Arkansas City, KS 67005
www.cowley.edu

Louisiana

Delgado Community College
Hospitality Program
615 City Park Ave.
New Orleans, LA 70119
www.dcc.edu

Nicholls State University
Culinary Arts
P.O. Box 2014
Thibodaux, LA 70310
www.nicholls.edu

Southern University
Hospitality Operations, Food and Beverage Management
3050 Martin Luther King Jr. Dr.
Shreveport, LA 71107
www.susla.edu

Maine

Andover College
Travel and Hospitality Management
901 Washington Ave.
Portland, ME 04103
www.andovercollege.edu

Southern Maine Community College
Culinary Arts
2 Fort Road
South Portland, ME 04106
www.smccme.edu

York County Community College
Lodging Operations, Food and Beverage Operations
112 College Dr.
Wells, ME 04090
www.yccc.edu

Maryland

Allegany Community College
Hotel/Motel Management
12402 Willow Brook Rd. SE
Cumberland, MD 21502
www.ac.cc.md.us

Anne Arundel Community College
Hotel, Restaurant Management
101 College Parkway C-205
Arnold, MD 21012
www.aacc.cc.md.us

Baltimore City Community College
Hospitality Management Program
2901 Liberty Heights Ave.
Baltimore, MD 21215
www.bccc.md.state.us

Baltimore's International Culinary College
School of Hospitality and Business Management
Commerce Exchange
17 Commerce St.
Baltimore, MD 21202
www.bic.edu

Montgomery College
Hospitality Management
51 Mannakee St.
Rockville, MD 20850
www.mc.cc.md.us

Wor-Wic Tech Community College
Hotel-Motel-Restaurant Management
32000 Campus Dr.
Salisbury, MD 21804
www.worwic.cc.md.us

Massachusetts

Bay State College
Travel and Hospitality Management
Boston, MA 02116
www.baystate.edu

Berkshire Community College
Hospitality Administration
1350 West St.
Pittsfield, MA 01201
www.cc.berkshire.org

Bunker Hill Community College
Hotel, Restaurant, Travel Program
250 New Rutherford Ave.
Boston, MA 02129
www.bhcc.mass.edu

Cape Cod Community College
Hotel Restaurant Management
Department of Business
2240 Iyanough Rd.
West Barnstable, MA 02668
www.capecod.mass.edu

Endicott College
Hospitality and Tourism
376 Hale St.
Beverly, MA 01915
www.endicott.edu

Gibbs College–Boston
Hospitality Management
126 Newbury St.
Boston, MA 02116
www.gibbsboston.edu

Holyoke Community College
Hospitality/Culinary Arts
303 Homestead Ave.
Holyoke, MA 01040
www.hcc.mass.edu

Marian Court College
Hospitality Management
35 Little's Point Rd.
Swampscott, MA 01907
www.mariancourt.edu

Massachusetts Bay Community College
Hospitality Management
19 Flagg Dr.
Framingham, MA 01702
www.massbay.edu

Massasoit Community College
Hotel and Restaurant Management
1 Massasoit Blvd.
Brockton, MA 02302
www.massasoit.mass.edu

Middlesex Community College
Hospitality Management
33 Kearney Sq.
Lowell, MA 01852
www.middlesex.mass.edu

Mount Ida College
Hotel and Tourism Management
777 Dedham St.
Newton, MA 02459
www.mountida.edu

Newbury College
Saunders School of Hotel and Restaurant Management
129 Fisher Ave.
Brookline, MA 02445
www.newbury.edu

North Shore Community College
Tourism/Hospitality Program
1 Ferncroft Rd.
Danvers, MA 01923
www.northshore.edu

Northern Essex Community College
Hotel and Restaurant Management
Elliott Way
Haverhill, MA 01830
www.necc.mass.edu

Quinsigamond Community College
Hotel and Restaurant Management
670 W. Boylston St.
Worcester, MA 01606
www.qcc.mass.edu

Michigan

Grand Rapids Community College
Hospitality Education
143 Bostwick NE
Grand Rapids, MI 49503
www.grcc.cc.mi.us

Henry Ford Community College
Hotel, Restaurant and Institutional Management
5101 Evergreen Rd.
Dearborn, MI 48128
www.henryford.cc.mi.us

Lake Michigan College
Hospitality Management
2755 E. Napier Ave.
Benton Harbor, MI 49022
www.lakemichigancollege.edu

Macomb Community College
Culinary Arts
14500 E. 12 Mile Rd.
Warren, MI 48088
www.macomb.edu

Northern Michigan University
Food Service Management
1401 Presque Isle Ave.
Marquette, MI 49855
www.nmu.edu

Northwestern Michigan College
Culinary Arts
1701 E. Front St.
Traverse City, MI 49686
www.nmc.edu

Oakland Community College
Hotel and Restaurant Management/Culinary Arts
2840 Opdyke Rd.
Bloomfield Hills, MI 48304
www.oaklandcc.edu

Washtenaw Community College
Culinary and Hospitality Management
4800 E. Huron River Dr.
P.O. Box D-1
Ann Arbor, MI 48106
www.wccnet.edu

Minnesota

Alexandria Technical College
Hotel-Restaurant Management
1601 Jefferson St.
Alexandria, MN 56308
www.alextech.edu

Minneapolis Community and Technical College
Culinary Arts
1415 Hennepin Ave.
Minneapolis, MN 55403
www.mctc.mnscu.edu

Normandale Community College
Hospitality Management
9700 France Ave. South
Bloomington, MN 55431
www.nr.cc.mn.us

Rainy River Community College
Hospitality Management Program
1501 Hwy. 71
International Falls, MN 56649
www.rrcc.mnscu.edu

University of Minnesota–Crookston
Hotel, Restaurant, and Institutional Management
Crookston, MN 56716
www.umcrookston.edu

Mississippi

Hinds Community College
Hotel and Restaurant Administration
Jackson, MS 39213
www.hindscc.edu

Meridian Community College
Hotel/Restaurant Management Technology
910 Hwy. 19 North
Meridian, MS 39307
www.mcc.cc.ms.us

Northeast Mississippi Community College
Hotel and Restaurant Management
101 Cunningham Blvd.
Booneville, MS 38829
www.necc.cc.ms.us

Northwest Mississippi Community College
Hotel and Restaurant Management Technology
Senatobia, MS 38668
www.northwestms.edu

Missouri

East Central College
Hospitality Program
1964 Prairie Dell Rd.
Union, MO 63084
www.eastcentral.edu

Jefferson College
Culinary Arts
Area Technical School
1000 Viking Dr.
Hillsboro, MO 63050
www.jeffco.edu

Metropolitan Community Colleges
Hospitality Management
Penn Valley Community College
3200 Broadway
Kansas City, MO 64111
http://kcmetro.edu

Ozarks Technology Community College
Hospitality Management
P.O. Box 5959
Springfield, MO 65801
www.otc.cc.mo.us

St. Louis Community College–Forest Park
Hospitality/Tourism Program
5600 Oakland Ave.
St. Louis, MO 63110
www.stlcc.cc.mo.us

Montana

Flathead Valley Community College
Hospitality Management Program
777 Grandview Ave.
Kalispell, MT 59901
www.fvcc.edu

Nebraska

Central Community College
Hotel, Motel, and Restaurant Services Program
Hastings, NE 68901
www.ccneb.edu

Southeast Community College
Foodservice/Hospitality Program
8800 O St.
Lincoln, NE 68520
www.southeast.edu

Nevada

Truckee Meadows Community College
Culinary Arts
7000 Dandini Blvd.
Reno, NV 89512
www.tmcc.edu

New Hampshire

New Hampshire Technical College
Restaurant Management
2020 Riverside Dr.
Berlin, NH 03570
www.nhctc.edu

Southern New Hampshire University
School of Hospitality
2500 N. River Rd.
Manchester, NH 03106
www.snhu.edu

New Jersey

Atlantic Community College
Food Service Management, Hospitality Specialist
Black Horse Pike, Rte. 322
Mays Landing, NJ 08330
www.atlantic.edu

Bergen Community College
Hospitality Management
Department of Business
400 Paramus Rd.
Paramus, NJ 07652
www.bergen.cc.nj.us

Burlington County College
Food Service and Hospitality Management
County Rte. 530
Pemberton, NJ 08068
www.bcc.edu

Gibbs College–Livingston
Hotel/Restaurant Management
630 W. Mount Pleasant Ave., Rte. 10
Livingston, NJ 07039
www.gibbsnj.edu

Mercer County Community College
Hotel, Restaurant, and Institution Management
North Broad St.
Trenton, NJ 06808
www.mccc.edu

Middlesex County College
Hotel, Restaurant, and Institution Management
2600 Woodbridge Ave.
P.O. Box 3050
Edison, NJ 08818
www.middlesexcc.edu

Union County College
Restaurant Management Program
1033 Springfield Ave.
Cranford, NJ 07016
www.ucc.edu

New Mexico

Doña Ana Branch Community College
Hospitality Services Program
Business and Information Systems Division
MSC 3DA
P.O. Box 30001
Las Cruces, NM 88003
http://dabcc-www.nmsu.edu

New York

Adirondack Community College
Foodservice Program, Hospitality, and Tourism Management
Bay Rd.
Queensbury, NY 12804
www.sunyacc.edu

Broome Community College
Hotel/Restaurant Management Program
Upper Front St., Rte. 11
Binghamton, NY 13902
www.sunybroome.edu

Bryant & Stratton College
Hotel and Restaurant Management Program
953 James St.
Syracuse, NY 13203
www.bryantstratton.edu

Culinary Institute of America
Foodservice Management
1946 Campus Dr.
Hyde Park, NY 12538
www.ciachef.edu

Erie Community College North
Hotel Restaurant Management
6205 Main St.
Williamsville, NY 14221
www.ecc.edu

Finger Lakes Community College
Hotel and Resort Management
4355 Lakeshore Dr.
Canandaigua, NY 14424
www.fingerlakes.edu

Genesee Community College
Hospitality Management
1 College Rd.
Batavia, NY 14020
www.genesee.edu

Herkimer County Community College
Travel and Tourism: Hospitality and Events Management
Business/Computer Division
Reservoir Rd.
Herkimer, NY 13350
www.hccc.ntcnet.com

Jefferson Community College
Hospitality and Tourism
Outer Coffeen St.
Watertown, NY 13601
www.sunyjefferson.edu

Katharine Gibbs School
Hotel and Restaurant Management
50 W. 40th St.
New York, NY 10018
www.gibbsny.edu

Mohawk Valley Community College
Culinary Arts and Restaurant Management
Upper Floyd Ave.
Rome, NY 13440
www.mvcc.edu

Monroe College
Hospitality Management and Culinary Arts
434 Main St.
New Rochelle, NY 10801
www.monroecollege.edu

Monroe Community College
Hotel and Hospitality Management
1000 W. Henrietta Rd.
Rochester, NY 14623
www.monroecc.edu

Nassau Community College
Hotel and Restaurant Technology
1 Education Dr.
Garden City, NY 11530
www.ncc.edu

New York City College of Technology
Hospitality Management
300 Jay St.
Brooklyn, NY 11201
www.citytech.cuny.edu

New York Institute of Technology
Culinary Arts
P.O. Box 9029
Central Islip, NY 11722
www.nyit.edu

Onondaga Community College
Foodservice Administration/Hotel Technology
4941 Onandaga Rd.
Syracuse, NY 13215
www.sunyocc.edu

Paul Smith's College
Hospitality Program
Rte. 86 & 30
P.O. Box 265
Paul Smiths, NY 12970
www.paulsmiths.edu

Rockland Community College
Hospitality and Tourism
145 College Rd.
Suffern, NY 10901
www.sunyrockland.edu

Schenectady County Community College
Hotel, Culinary Arts, and Tourism
78 Washington Ave.
Schenectady, NY 12305
www.sunysccc.edu

SUNY Cobleskill
Culinary Arts, Hospitality, and Tourism
Cobleskill, NY 12043
www.cobleskill.edu

SUNY Delhi
Hospitality Management
2 Main St.
Delhi, NY 13753
www.delhi.edu

Suffolk County Community College
Culinary Arts
Riverhead, NY 11901
www.sunysuffolk.edu

Sullivan County Community College
Hospitality Management, Food Service Program
www.sullivan.suny.edu

Trocaire College
Hospitality Management Program
360 Choate Ave.
Buffalo, NY 14220
www.trocaire.edu

Westchester Community College
Food Service Administration
75 Grasslands Rd.
Valhalla, NY 10595
www.sunywcc.edu

North Carolina

Asheville-Buncombe Technical College
Hotel and Restaurant Management, Culinary Technology
340 Victoria Rd.
Asheville, NC 28801
www.asheville.cc.nc.us

Cape Fear Community College
Hotel and Restaurant Management, Culinary Technology
411 N. Front St.
Wilmington, NC 28401
http://cfcc.edu

Central Piedmont Community College
Hospitality Education
P.O. Box 35009
Charlotte, NC 28235
www.cpcc.cc.nc.us

Sandhills Community College
Hotel and Restaurant Management Program
2200 Airport Rd.
Pinehurst, NC 28734
www.sandhills.cc.nc.us

Wake Technical Community College
Hotel and Restaurant Management, Culinary Technology
9101 Fayetteville Rd.
Raleigh, NC 27603
www.wake.tec.nc.us

Wilkes Community College
Hotel, Restaurant Management
Drawer 120
Wilkesboro, NC 28697
www.wilkes.cc.nc.us

North Dakota

Bismarck State College
Hotel-Restaurant Management
1500 Edwards Ave.
P.O. Box 5587
Bismarck, ND 58506
www.bsc.nodak.edu

North Dakota State College of Science
Culinary Arts
800 Sixth St. North
Wahpeton, ND 58076
www.ndscs.nodak.edu

Ohio

Cincinnati State Technical and Community College
Hotel and Food Service Management
3520 Central Pkwy.
Cincinnati, OH 45223
www.cinstate.cc.oh.us

Columbus State Community College
Hospitality Management
550 E. Spring St.
Columbus, OH 43215
http://cscc.edu

Cuyahoga Community College
Hospitality Management
700 Carnegie Ave.
Cleveland, OH 44115
www.tri-c.edu

Hocking Technical College
School of Hospitality
3301 Hocking Pkwy.
Nelsonville, OH 45764
www.hocking.edu

Lakeland Community College
Hotel Management and Culinary Arts Technology
7700 Clocktown Dr.
Kirtland, OH 44094
www.lakeland.cc.oh.us

Oklahoma

Carl Albert State College
Hotel/Restaurant and Tourism Management
1507 S. Mckenna
Poteau, OK 74953
www.carlalbert.edu

Oklahoma State University–Okmulgee
Hospitality Services
1801 E. 4th St.
Okmulgee, OK 74447
www.osu-okmulgee.edu

Oregon

Central Oregon Community College
Hospitality and Tourism Management, Culinary Institute
2600 NW College Way
Bend, OR 97701
www.cocc.edu

Chemeketa Community College
Hotel, Restaurant, and Resort Management
Cooley Dr. NE
Salem, OR 97309
www.chemek.cc.or.us

Lane Community College
Hospitality/Culinary Arts
4000 E. 30th Ave.
Eugene, OR 97405
www.lanecc.edu

Linn-Benton Community College
Culinary Arts
6500 Pacific Blvd. SW
Albany, OR 97321
www.linnbenton.edu

Mt. Hood Community College
Hospitality and Tourism Management
26000 SE Stark St.
Gresham, OR 97030
www.mhcc.edu

Pennsylvania

Bucks County Community College
Hospitality Tourism Management, Food Service Management
Swamp Rd.
Newton, PA 18940
www.bucks.edu

Butler County Community College
Hospitality Management
P.O. Box 1203
Butler, PA 16003
http://bc3.cc.pa.us/index.htm

Central Pennsylvania College
Hotel and Restaurant Management
College Hill and Valley Rds.
Summerdale, PA 17093
www.centralpenn.edu

Community College of Allegheny County
Hotel-Restaurant Management
595 Beatty Rd.
Monroeville, PA 15146
www.ccac.edu

Community College of Philadelphia
Hotel and Restaurant Management, Culinary Management
1700 Spring Garden St.
Philadelphia, PA 19130
www.ccp.edu

Harrisburg Area Community College
Restaurant Operations
1 HACC Dr.
Harrisburg, PA 17110
www.hacc.edu

Indiana University of Pennsylvania
Culinary Arts
1011 South Dr.
Indiana, PA 15705
www.iup.edu

Keystone Junior College
Hotel and Restaurant Management
1 College Green
La Plume, PA 18440
www.keystone.edu

Lehigh Carbon Community College
Hotel/Restaurant Management, Culinary Arts
4525 Education Park Dr.
Schnecksville, PA 18078
www.lccc.edu

Luzerne County Community College
Hotel and Restaurant Management, Culinary Arts
1333 S. Prospect St.
Nanticoke, PA 18634
www.luzerne.edu

Montgomery County Community College
Hotel and Restaurant Management, Culinary Arts
340 Dekalb Pike
Bluebell, PA 19422
www.mc3.edu

Northampton Community College
Hotel/Restaurant Management, Culinary Arts
3835 Green Pond Rd.
Bethlehem, PA 18020
www.northampton.edu

Pennsylvania College of Technology
Hospitality Management, Culinary Arts Technology
1 College Ave.
Williamsport, PA 17701
www.pct.edu

Pennsylvania Culinary Institute
717 Liberty Ave.
Pittsburgh, PA 15222
www.pci.edu

Pittsburgh Technical Institute
Hospitality Management Administration
635 Smithfield St.
Pittsburgh, PA 15222
www.pti.edu

The Restaurant School–Walnut Hill College
Restaurant, Hotel Management, Culinary Institute
4207 Walnut St.
Philadelphia, PA 19104
www.therestaurantschool.com

Westmoreland County Community College
Hotel/Motel Management, Culinary Arts
College Station Rd.
Youngwood, PA 15697
http://wccc-pa.edu

Widener University
School of Hospitality Management
1 University Pl.
Chester, PA 19103
www.widener.edu

Rhode Island

Johnson & Wales University
Hospitality Management/Culinary Arts
8 Abbott Park Pl.
Providence, RI 02903
www.jwu.edu

South Carolina

Greenville Technical College
Culinary Education
P.O. Box 5616
Greenville, SC 29606
www.greenvilletech.com

Horry-Georgetown Technical College
Hospitality/Tourism Management
2050 Hwy. 501 East
P.O. Box 261966
Conway, SC 29528
www.hgtc.edu

Johnson & Wales University
Culinary Education, Hospitality Department
701 E. Bay St.
Charleston, SC 29403
www.jwu.edu/charles

Trident Technical College
Hospitality, Tourism, and Culinary Arts
P.O. Box 118067
Charleston, SC 29423
www.tridenttech.edu

South Dakota

Black Hills State University
Tourism and Hospitality
College of Business and Technology
1200 University St., Unit 9502
Spearfish, SD 57799
www.bhsu.edu

Mitchell Technical Institute
Culinary Academy
821 N. Capital St.
Mitchell, SD 57301
www.mitchelltech.com

Tennessee

Southwest Tennessee Community College
Hospitality Management
3833 Mountain Terr.
Memphis, TN 38127
www.southwest.tn.edu

Volunteer State Community College
Hospitality/Restaurant Management Program
1480 Nashville Pike
Gallatin, TN 37066
www.vscc.cc.tn.us

Texas

Austin Community College
Hospitality Management, Culinary Arts
5930 Middle Fiskville Rd.
Austin, TX 78752
www.austin.cc.tx.us

Central Texas College
Hospitality Management
P.O. Box 1800
Killeen, TX 76540
www.ctcd.edu

Collin County Community College
Hotel/Restaurant Management
2200 W. University Dr.
McKinney, TX 75070
www.ccccd.edu

Del Mar College
Hotel/Motel Management, Culinary Arts
101 Baldwin Rd.
Corpus Christi, TX 78404
www.delmar.edu

El Centro College
Food and Hospitality Services
801 Main St.
Dallas, TX 75202
www.ecc.dcccd.edu

Galveston College
Culinary/Hospitality Management
4015 Ave. Q
Galveston, TX 77550
www.gc.edu

Houston Community College
Hotel/Restaurant Management
3100 Main at Elgin
Houston, TX 77002
www.hccs.edu

St. Phillip's College
Hotel Management, Culinary Arts
1801 Martin Luther King Dr.
San Antonio, TX 78203
www.accd.edu

Utah

Dixie College
Hospitality Management Program
225 S. 700 E St.
St. George, UT 84770
www.dixie.edu

Utah Valley State College
Hospitality Management, Culinary Arts
800 W. University Pkwy.
Orem, UT 84058
www.uvsc.edu

Vermont

Champlain College
Hotel/Restaurant Management
163 S. Willard St.
Burlington, VT 05401
www.champlain.edu

New England Culinary Institute
Culinary Arts
250 Main St.
Montpelier, VT 05602
www.neci.edu

Virginia

J. Sargeant Reynolds Community College
Culinary Arts, Tourism, and Hospitality Program
P.O. Box 85622
Richmond, VA 23285
www.jsr.cc.va.us

Northern Virginia Community College
Hospitality Management, Culinary Arts
8333 Little River Turnpike
Annandale, VA 22003
www.nv.cc.va.us

Washington

Highline Community College
Hotel and Tourism Management
2400 S. 240th St.
Des Moines, WA 98198
www.highline.edu

Lake Washington Technical College
Hotel Services and Operations, Culinary Arts
11605 132nd Ave. NE
Kirkland, WA 98034
www.lwtc.ctc.edu

Northwest Indian College
Hotel and Restaurant Management Program
2522 Kwina Rd.
Bellingham, WA 98226
www.nwic.edu

Olympic College
Culinary Arts
1600 Chester Ave.
Bremerton, WA 98337
www.olympic.edu

Skagit Valley College
Culinary Arts and Hospitality Management
2405 E. College Way
Mount Vernon, WA 98273
www.skagit.edu

South Seattle Community College
Culinary Arts
6000 16th Ave. SW
Seattle, WA 98106
www.southseattle.edu

Spokane Community College
Hotel and Restaurant Management, Culinary Arts
1810 N. Greene St.
Spokane, WA 99217
www.scc.spokane.edu

Yakima Valley Community College
Hospitality/Tourism Program
16th and Nob Hill Rd.
Yakima, WA 98907
www.yvcc.edu

West Virginia

West Virginia Northern Community College
Hotel and Restaurant Management Program
1704 Market St.
Wheeling, WV 26003
www.northern.wvnet.edu

Wisconsin

Chippewa Valley Technical College
Hotel and Restaurant Management
620 W. Clairemont Ave.
Eau Claire, WI 54701
www.cvtc.edu

Fox Valley Technical College
Hotel and Restaurant Management, Culinary Arts
1825 N. Bluemound Dr.
P.O. Box 2277
Appleton, WI 54912
www.foxvalley.tec.wi.us

Gateway Technical College
Hotel/Hospitality Management, Culinary Arts
1001 S. Main St.
Racine, WI 53403
www.gtc.edu

Madison Area Technical College
Hotel and Restaurant Management, Culinary Arts
3550 Anderson St.
Madison, WI 53704
http://matcmadison.edu

Milwaukee Area Technical College
Hotel/Hospitality Management, Culinary Arts
700 W. State St.
Milwaukee, WI 53233
www.milwaukee.tec.wi.us

Moraine Park Technical College
Culinary Arts
700 Gould St.
Beaver Dam, WI
www.moraine.tec.wi.us

Nicolet Area Technical College
Food Service Management
P.O. Box 518
County Hwy. G
Rhinelander, WI 54501
www.nicolet.tec.wi.us

Waukesha County Technical College
Hospitality and Culinary Center
800 Main St.
Pewaukee, WI 53072
www.wctc.edu

Wyoming

Sheridan College
Hospitality Management Program
P.O. Box 1500
Sheridan, WY 82801
www.sheridan.edu

Educational Programs in Canada

Alberta

Southern Alberta Institute of Technology
1301 16th Ave. NW
Calgary, AB T2M 0L4
www.sait.ca

Univeristy of Calgary
Haskayne School of Business
351 Scurfield Hall
215 Campus Pl. NW
Calgary, AB T2N 1N4
www.ucalgary.ca

British Columbia

Malaspina University-College
900 Fifth St.
Nanaimo, BC V9R 5S5
www.mala.ca

Thompson Rivers University
4355 Mathissi Pl.
Burnaby, BC V5G 4S8
www.openlearning.tru.ca

Thompson Rivers University
Tourism Management Department
Box 3010
Kamloops, BC V2C 5N3
www.tru.ca

University of Victoria
Bachelor of Commerce Program
P.O. Box 1700 STN CSC
Victoria, BC V8W 2Y2
www.uvic.ca

Manitoba

University of Manitoba
102 Frank Kennedy Centre
Faculty of Physical Education & Recreation Studies
Winnipeg, MB R3T 2N2
www.umanitoba.ca

New Brunswick

University of New Brunswick in Saint John
Faculty of Business
P.O. Box 5050
Saint John, NB E2L 4L5
www.unbsj.ca

Nova Scotia

Mount Saint Vincent University
166 Bedford Hwy.
Halifax, NS B3M 2J6
www.msvu.ca

University College of Cape Breton
P.O. Box 5300
1250 Grand Lake Rd.
Sydney, NS B1P 6L2
www.capebretonu.ca

Ontario

Brock University
500 Glenridge Ave.
St. Catharines, ON L2S 3A1
www.brocku.ca

Ryerson University
350 Victoria St.
Toronto, ON M5B 2K3
www.ryerson.ca

University of Guelph
Admission Services
Office of Registrarial Services
Third Fl., University Centre
Guelph, ON N1G 2W1
www.uoguelph.ca

University of Waterloo
Faculty of Environmental Studies
200 University Ave. West
Waterloo, ON N2L 3G1
www.uwaterloo.ca

Québec

Université Laval
Bureau d'information et de promotion
2435 Pavillon Jean-Charles-Bonenfant
Québec City, QC G1K 7P4
www.ulaval.ca

Appendix B

Professional Associations

The following is a list of national associations to contact for further information on opportunities in the hotel/motel and hospitality industries.

U.S. Associations

American Hotel and Lodging Association
1201 New York Ave. NW, Ste. 600
Washington, DC 20005
www.ahla.com

Council of Hotel and Restaurant Trainers (CHART)
P.O. Box 835
Westfield, NJ 07091
www.chart.org

The Hospitality and Information Service
Meridian House
1630 Crescent Pl. NW
Washington, DC 20009
www.this4diplomats.org

Hospitality Information Technology Association
www.hitaworld.org

Hospitality Sales and Marketing Association International
8201 Greensboro Dr.
McLean, VA 22102
www.hsmai.org

National Association of Black Hotel Owners, Operators, and
    Developers, Inc. (NABHOOD)
3520 W. Broward Blvd., Ste. 218B
Ft. Lauderdale, FL 33312
www.nabhood.org

National Restaurant Association
Educational Foundation
1200 Seventeenth St. NW
Washington, DC 20036
www.restaurant.org

Professional Association of Innkeepers International
16 S. Haddon Ave.
Haddonfield, NJ 08033
www.pai.org

Canadian Associations

Canadian Culinary Federation
www.ccfcc.ca

Canadian Restaurant and Foodservices Association
316 Bloor St. West
Toronto, ON M5S 1W5
www.crfa.ca

Hotel Association of Canada
130 Albert St., Ste. 1206
Ottawa, ON K1P 5G4
www.hotelassociation.ca

Appendix C

Periodicals

Condé Nast Traveler
www.cntraveller.com

Cornell Hotel & Restaurant Administration Quarterly
www.hotelschool.cornell.edu/publications/hraq

Hospitality Upgrade
www.hotel-online.com

Hotel Business
www.hotelbusiness.com

Hotel & Motel Management
www.hotelmotel.com

HSMAI Marketing Review
www.hsmai.org/resources/review.cfm

Lodging Hospitality
www.lhonline.com

Lodging Magazine
www.lodgingmagazine.com

Meetings & Conventions
www.meetings-conventions.com

Nation's Restaurant News
www.nrn.com

Restaurant Business
www.restaurantbusiness.com

Successful Meetings
www.successmtgs.com

Travel & Leisure
www.travelandleisure.com

About the Author

SHEPARD HENKIN HAD a varied and distinguished career in the hotel industry, serving with many highly regarded hotels and chains. His positions included marketing, public relations management, operations, acquisitions, profit-center supervision, and consulting services.

For eleven years, Henkin was vice president in charge of marketing for Loews Hotels, a major international hotel chain. He had been president and chief operating officer of Association Services, Inc., a Washington, DC–based hotel consulting firm. In addition, he headed sales and promotional activities for the Governor Clinton Hotel in New York and for the twenty-five-hundred-room Hotel New Yorker. He also organized hotel and restaurant promotional programs for UMC Industries, a St. Louis, Missouri, conglomerate. Henkin was vice president, corporate sales, of Olympic Tower in New York, an unusual condominium complex conceived by Aristotle Onassis. He was also associated with Rockefeller Center, Inc.

Henkin attended Amherst College in Massachusetts and was a graduate of the University of Iowa in Iowa City. He also wrote another volume in this series, *Opportunities in Public Relations*.

This edition has been thoroughly revised by Josephine Scanlon, a writer and editor with expertise in career information.